An Irrepressible Conflict

THE SIEGE OF PETERSBURG
This print by the New York printmakers Currier & Ives depicts one of the final battles around Petersburg. Unlike many of their earlier works, individuals are subsumed by the anonymity of the mass of humanity that the Civil War armies had become by 1865. *(Library of Congress)*

AN IRREPRESSIBLE

CONFLICT

THE EMPIRE STATE IN THE CIVIL WAR

Robert Weible, Jennifer A. Lemak, and Aaron Noble

With a Foreword by Harold Holzer

excelsior editions

AN IMPRINT OF STATE UNIVERSITY OF NEW YORK PRESS

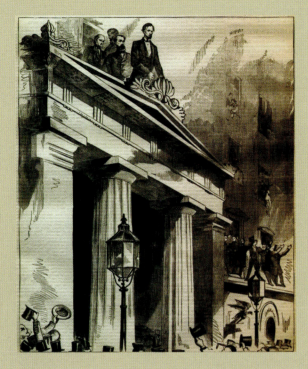

Lincoln in New York City
At each stop along his route, the President-elect was greeted
by large, cheering crowds. In New York City, Lincoln remarked to
Mayor Wood his gratitude for the reception even in a city whose
citizens "do not by a majority agree with me in political sentiments."
(New York State Library, Manuscripts and Special Collections)

page i: **Flank Marker** of the 132nd New York Volunteer
Infantry Regiment, part of which was recruited from the Allegany,
Cattaraugus, and Tuscarora Reservations.
(New York State Military Museum, Division of Military and Naval Affairs)

Published by
STATE UNIVERSITY OF NEW YORK PRESS, ALBANY

© 2014 The New York State Education Department, Albany, NY 12230
All rights reserved

Printed in the United States of America

EXCELSIOR EDITIONS
is an imprint of State University of New York Press.

For information, contact
State University of New York Press, Albany, NY
www.sunypress.edu

Production and book design, Laurie Searl
Marketing, Kate R. Seburyamo

Library of Congress Cataloging-in-Publication Data

Weible, Robert.
  An irrepressible conflict : the Empire State in the Civil War / Robert Weible, Jennifer
A. Lemak, Aaron Noble ; foreword by Harold Holzer.
      pages cm — (Excelsior editions)
  Includes bibliographical references and index.
  ISBN 978-1-4384-5348-4 (paperback : alkaline paper) 1. New York (State)—
History)—Civil War, 1861–1865—Exhibitions. 2. New York (State)—History—Civil
War, 1861–1865—Sources—Exhibitions. 3. New York (State)—History—Civil War,
1861–1865—Pictorial works—Exhibitions. 4. United States—History—Civil War,
1861–1865—Sources—Exhibitions. 5. United States—History—Civil War, 1861–1865—
Pictorial works—Exhibitions. I. Lemak, Jennifer A. II. Noble, Aaron. III. Title.
E523.W45 2014
973.7'447—dc23   2014001945

10 9 8 7 6 5 4 3 2 1

Contents

Miniature soldier, cast metal, painted, c. 1950
(New York State Museum Collection, H-1967.2.85)

EARLY DUTCH SLAVERY IN NEW YORK STATE

(New York Public Library)

Director's Message

Mark Schaming

When Americans think about the Civil War, they are most likely to recall the great battlefields of the conflict—Manassas, Antietam, or Gettysburg. Few would immediately recognize the critical role that the State of New York and its citizens played in the struggle for the nation's soul. It was in response to this challenge that the New York State Museum's exhibition team in conjunction with our partners in the New York State Archives and Library began development of "An Irrepressible Conflict: The Empire State in the Civil War." The New York State Board of Regents has, through their vision, moved the State Museum to develop exhibitions and educational programs designed to educate all New Yorkers in meaningful ways. "An Irrepressible Conflict" is an important expression of this vision.

The American Civil War was an enormously complex network of people and events, which provides us a platform to better understand who and where we are today. At the time of the War, the nation was undergoing enormous and divergent change. Along with the political, social, and economic causes that led to war, this was an era of both enlightenment and ignorance, as the United States became a more culturally aware nation, with an increasing awareness about our place in the world. New York State was at the center of most of these significant political, social, cultural, and political movements.

There is no singular stream in the course of events that constructs a linear historical narrative. The exhibition, and this publication, relied on the research, collections, and reflections of many. Grounding its interpretation in the latest professional scholarship, the planning team determined that the exhibit would take a long view, from the beginning of New York as a slave state four hundred years ago through the civil rights era of the 1960s. As a program of the New York State Education Department,

CIVIL RIGHTS PROTEST PIN, CIRCA 1960s
(Elizabeth Meaders Collection)

the mission of the New York State Museum is to raise the knowledge, skill, and opportunity of all the people in New York. In order to accomplish this mission, the planning team sought to engage New Yorkers from across the state by reaching out to museums, libraries, and historical societies statewide. The response was impressive and eventually over two dozen institutions and individuals loaned objects, documents, or photographs to the exhibition, whose title was drawn from an 1858 speech in Rochester by New York Senator William Seward. We are indebted to the great museums across the state that loaned the artifacts and provided scholarship that reflect on New York's role in this important chapter in American history. We are especially grateful for the guidance and assistance of Harold Holzer. He has, for these important years that mark the war, shaped our collective understanding of the people and events that changed the country.

Through this unprecedented spirit of cooperation, "An Irrepressible Conflict" details the important perspective of New York's central role in the Civil War by telling the story of New Yorkers from every corner of the state—and the exhibition was richer for it. This catalogue encompasses the stories told throughout "An Irrepressible Conflict" as well as several compelling new additions that, for want of gallery space, we were not able to share in the museum's exhibition.

MARK SCHAMING
Director, New York State Museum

Foreword

New York and Lincoln's First Step to Freedom

Harold Holzer

Late in 1863, Abraham Lincoln received an unexpected request from New York State's capital—a request, it is fair to say, that he probably wished had never arrived. Yet once he granted it, his decision ensured the physical preservation of what he called "the central act of my Administration and the great event of the nineteenth century."[1] And it launched New York's unwavering commitment to enshrining its Civil War legacy and sharing it with the public.

It seemed that the organizers of the forthcoming Albany Army Relief Association Fair hoped that Lincoln might consider donating the one and only copy of the Emancipation Proclamation remaining in his control: the so-called "Preliminary Proclamation," issued September 22, 1862, which gave the Confederacy one hundred days' notice to end its rebellion or forfeit its slaves "thenceforward, and forever."[2] The fair managers proposed to raffle off the icon, and use the funds it generated to aid wounded soldiers. Lincoln's priceless relic would undoubtedly become the star attraction at the event.

Could the President resist such a request? He certainly tried. Just a year earlier, the organizers of a similar event in Chicago had persuaded Lincoln to part with the handwritten manuscript of his *final*, January 1, 1863, proclamation, but its donation had required the repeated importuning of several Illinois political allies. Now he had but one emancipation proclamation left in his possession, and he was reluctant to part with it for any reason. Once again, it took considerable arm-twisting to get the author of the

---

1. Frank [Francis] B. Carpenter, "Anecdotes and Reminiscences," in Henry J. Raymond, *The Life and Public Services of Abraham Lincoln* (New York: Derby & Miller, 1865), 764.

2. From the text of the Preliminary Emancipation Proclamation, September 22, 1862, in Roy P. Basler, ed., *The Collected Works of Abraham Lincoln*, 8 vols. (New Brunswick, NJ: Rutgers University Press, 1953–1955), 5:434.

19   ABRAHAM LINCOLN
The Cooper Institute photograph, by
M. B. Brady, New York, February 27, 1860.

ABRAHAM LINCOLN
This photograph of Lincoln was taken by Mathew Brady during Lincoln's visit to New York City in 1860. *(New York State Library, Manuscripts and Special Collections)*

most important freedom document of the century to donate his handiwork.

Then why did he comply? The original request came from an official named William Barnes, the state superintendent of insurance, who enjoyed no particular relationship with the president, but boasted one important claim to attention from the White House. Barnes was married to the daughter of Albany newspaper titan Thurlow Weed, the state's Republican Party boss and an influential wire-puller known as "The Wizard of the Lobby." Thus, not for the first or last time, a lobbyist managed in the end to persuade a high-ranking official to do something he did not particularly want to do—or at least found a way around his opposition. To accomplish her mission, Mrs. Barnes, Weed's daughter, wrote directly to her father's longtime ally, Secretary of State William H. Seward, a New Yorker, and asked him to press the case for the donation. Much of the subsequent correspondence is lost, but clearly it succeeded. On January 4, 1864, Seward's office sent Mrs. Barnes what it proudly described as "the original draft of the September proclamation," noting, as if in explanation for its peculiar appearance, that the "body" of the work was "in his [Lincoln's] own handwriting."[3] The rest of it,

---

3. Frank [Francis] B. Carpenter, "Anecdotes and Reminiscences," in Henry J. Raymond, *The Life and Public Services of Abraham Lincoln* (New York: Derby & Miller, 1865), 764.

From the text of the Preliminary Emancipation Proclamation, September 22, 1862, in Roy P. Basler, ed., *The Collected Works of Abraham Lincoln*, 8 vols. (New Brunswick, NJ: Rutgers University Press, 1953–1955), 5:434.

F. W. Seward to Mrs. William Barnes, January 4, 1864, New York State Library, Manuscripts and Special Collections, 14977. For the full story of the episode and its meaning, see Loretta Ebert, "With the President's Permission: How New York State Acquired the Emancipation Proclamation," New York State Library, 9.

as Mr. and Mrs. Barnes would immediately notice, was comprised of excerpts from the printed version of the 1862 Congressional Confiscation Act, snipped and carefully glued onto the page by Lincoln himself—although, in one spot on the document, the president's fingerprint was clearly visible.

In truth, the sixteenth president's relations with the Empire State were not always as rosy as the request and deal for this extraordinary donation implied. After all, Lincoln had defeated New York's favorite son, Seward, to win the 1860 Republican nomination for president after making a stirring debut appearance at Manhattan's Cooper Union. Lincoln's subsequent convention triumph left many New York politicians angry and frustrated. On Election Day, however, the state gave Lincoln its thirty-five electoral votes and a strong fifty-thousand-vote popular plurality over his nearest rival.

But in the three years since, New York—like the nation itself—had become increasingly divided. Manhattan and Brooklyn remained overwhelmingly loyal to the Democratic Party and many of its citizens were opposed to the administration and the war, and particularly to freedom for enslaved African Americans. Lincoln's popularity may have held firm in upstate Republican strongholds, but it plummeted in the Democratic city of Albany, where his unprecedented use of executive power to quell dissent inspired an 1863 mass meeting chaired by local businessman-politician Erastus Corning. Corning then dispatched a strong letter of protest to the president, which was followed by a now-famous reply from Lincoln defending his efforts to put down the

rebellion even if it meant administering temporary "emetics" to the body politic—including the suspension of the writ of habeas corpus, and the imposition of arbitrary arrests, military trials for civilians, and newspaper suppression.[4]

Worse, in July 1863, the festering opposition to the Lincoln administration's policies boiled over in New York City just as federal officials there began selecting the names of the first enrollees under the new military draft. In violent response, Manhattan erupted in riots that brought death to scores of African Americans and the destruction of more than a million dollars' worth of property. "This is a time of humiliation for the country," diarist George Templeton Strong had observed early in the secession crisis. "We are a weak, divided, disgraced people, unable to maintain our national existence. We are impotent even to assert our national life."[5] Now the situation had become more divided still. Draft disturbances broke out in upstate cities as well.

Yet astoundingly, Lincoln proved willing by the end of that year to donate the most precious personal and historic relic in his care to a city that had never supported him and whose leading citizen, the governor, was anti-Lincoln Democrat Horatio Seymour, who, according to some critics, had tried legitimizing the Manhattan draft rioters by addressing them as his "friends." What had changed?

EMILY WEED BARNES, *left*
Signature card with a photograph of Emily Weed Barnes.
(New York State Library, Manuscripts and Special Collections)

---

4. See Lincoln's letter to Erastus Corning and others, June 12, 1863, *The Collected Works of Lincoln*, 6:260–69; an excellent article on the Corning affair is Frank J. Williams, "Civil Liberties in Wartime New York," in Harold Holzer, ed., *Lincoln and New York* (New York: New York Historical Society, 2009), 168–93.

5. Quoted in Harold Holzer, ed., *The Union Preserved: A Guide to Civil War Records in the New York State Archives* (New York: Fordham University Press, 1999), 7.

For one thing, another election was approaching. Lincoln would be seeking a second term as president, and hoped to keep New York's big trove of electoral votes in the Republican column. A gubernatorial election would take place as well, and Lincoln wanted nothing more than to see the Democrats' hold on the state's highest office terminated. But for another, New York, for all its pockets of political opposition and dissent, had responded heroically to the rebellion, quickly recruiting and arming more than 200,000 men for the army. By war's end in 1865, New York would send more than 448,000 men into the armed services—and mourn 53,000 casualties. No state provided more men, money, or materiel for the Union cause.

The state could also claim the first officer to die for the Union cause—Malta, New York–born Zouave colonel Ephraim Elmer Ellsworth. He was shot dead by an Alexandria, Virginia, innkeeper in May 1861 after ripping a large Confederate flag from atop a local hotel. New York also housed the all-important United States Military Academy at West Point, the high-tech Parrott Gun Foundry in Cold Spring, and the Brooklyn Navy Yard, which in 1862 outfitted the Union ironclad *Monitor*—constructed in part from metal forged at iron works in upstate Troy.

Perhaps in the end, Abraham Lincoln donated his Emancipation Proclamation to the Albany fair only as a personal favor to his powerful friends Thurlow Weed and William Seward. But one thing is sure: his decision also signaled his confidence that the largest state in the Union would somehow do its utmost to honor and preserve the talismanic relic. Needless to say, its arrival in Albany sparked huge interest in the event. Organizers took maximum advantage of the publicity it generated by delaying the raffle for the document until the final night of the wintertime fair, giving eager participants plenty of time to purchase one-dollar chances.

The organizers did make one audacious marketing blunder in the run-up to the raffle, announcing that they would draw the winning ticket from an authentic "draft wheel"—one that had actually been used to select the names of conscripts for the army. The impolitic reminder of the unpopular policy inspired a humorous, rhymed complaint in the fair's official newsletter to mark the arrival of the Preliminary Emancipation Proclamation:

> The President sent in a *Draft*—;
> What else could be expected,
> From one who's dealt in nothing else
> Ever since he was elected?[6]

In the end, the gibe did nothing to inhibit interest in the relic itself. As William Barnes pointed out to the wealthy New York abolitionist Geritt Smith, a member of the fair's organizing committee: "I think the 22nd Sept. is really more valuable than the 1st of Jany . . . The *Judgment* was really pronounced in Sept . . .The Sept. Proclamation first embodied the President's plan [and] . . . was really the effective Proclamation of Freedom."[7]

Apparently, Smith needed no further convincing. He proceeded to purchase a thousand one-dollar chances for the raffle, and when it was finally held on May 9, a "loud and hearty cheer" greeted the almost inevitable announcement that the man who had once helped to finance John Brown's raid had now

---

6. *Albany Canteen*, quoted in Harold Holzer, *Emancipating Lincoln: The Emancipation Proclamation in Text, Context, and Memory* (Cambridge, MA.: Harvard University Press, 2012), 116.

7. Quoted in Ebert, "With the President's Permission," 10–11.

won Lincoln's proclamation of freedom. "Everyone was satisfied," wrote Barnes. "The disposition of it although by chance is eminently just."[8]

Smith proved to be an extremely public-spirited custodian. He gave formal title to the relic to the US Sanitary Commission so it could be resold to raise even more money for the benefit of wounded soldiers, but in the end never authorized it to leave Albany. Meanwhile, Barnes pressed the state legislature to purchase the proclamation for New York. It finally did so, again for the price of $1,000, a few months after Lincoln's assassination in 1865. And ever since, the state has beautifully preserved the document. It has only gained in importance. Because Lincoln's January 1 final proclamation tragically burned in the Chicago Fire, the New York manuscript now holds the distinction of being the only surviving Emancipation Proclamation in Lincoln's hand.

To mark the 150th anniversary of its 1862 announcement, Chancellor Merryl H. Tisch of the New York State Board of Regents and Commissioner of Education John B. King Jr. called in 2012 for a statewide tour of the relic. Following visits to a number of upstate and downstate venues, the proclamation went on extended view at the opening of the New York State Museum's extraordinary exhibit devoted to the state's full and complex role in the Civil War. Of course, the proclamation was the most notable item on display, but it was one of many extraordinary treasures that greeted visitors during the show's long and successful run—as the pages of this catalogue will show—including the very flag Colonel Ellsworth seized in Alexandria.

New York's commitment to protecting and interpreting the Civil War remains unmatched, even by the standards of those states that witnessed the conflict's major battles. Its collections, its expertise, and its public outreach guarantee that visitors, readers, aficionados, students, and teachers enjoy ongoing access to the treasures we have so passionately collected and professionally preserved. I was honored to serve as a consultant to the recent New York State Museum exhibition, but the entire credit for the endeavor goes to Mark Schaming, the museum's innovative director, and to our hard-working state historian, Robert Weible. All of us have been inspired by Governor Andrew Cuomo's own passion for American and New York State history, and his mandate that our collections and sites be featured more prominently than ever.

Like William Barnes before them, they make sure that New York houses the greatest relics of our past so they can help us understand the present and prepare for the future. And they make sure that they are preserved, protected, and shared with all of us. One senses that Lincoln would have hoped for no better destiny for the document he treasured above all others.

HAROLD HOLZER
Senior Vice President for Public Affairs
The Metropolitan Museum of Art

---

8. William Barnes to Geritt Smith, March 17, 1864, Geritt Smith Papers, Arents Library, Syracuse University, microfilm copy in New York State Library.

PULPIT
This pulpit symbolizes the power and passion of the abolition movement in antebellum New York. Designed by famed architect Andrew Jackson Davis for the Holy Cross Church in Troy, Rensselaer County, the pulpit is similar to many found throughout New York, from which abolitionist preachers delivered fiery messages on the evils of slavery. *(New York State Museum Collection, H-2011.4.1)*

Introduction

Robert Weible

Theodore Roosevelt once told an audience of Civil War veterans that "there have been two great crises in our country's history: first when it was formed, and then, when it was perpetuated."[1] Roosevelt was himself a historian, and he was clearly on to something. His words are as true today as they were when he spoke them a century ago. Roosevelt was more than a historian, of course. He was also a proud New Yorker, and he would likely have agreed that there is no better way to view the second of America's two great crises—whether in the twentieth century or the twenty-first—than through the lens of New Yorkers who witnessed the Civil War firsthand and who forever keep its memory alive.

New Yorkers have, in fact, been keeping those memories alive and making sense of them ever since the war ended in 1865. Just look at the New York landscape. There are Civil War monuments and memorials everywhere: in town squares and city parks and along roadsides in every corner of the state. Or just consider the New Yorkers who, to this day, participate in Civil War Roundtables, research the lives of their Civil War ancestors, and read and write books and articles of scholarly and popular interest. And understand that when the Civil War Sesquicentennial got underway in 2011, New Yorkers—through local and regional historical societies and museums, state humanities council programs, and private initiatives—demonstrated their unshakable determination to honor the heroism of their forebears while also making the war relevant for today's audiences.

For its part, the New York State Museum developed a traveling exhibition entitled "The First Step to Freedom: Abraham Lincoln's Preliminary Emancipation Proclamation."

---

1. Theodore Roosevelt, "The New Nationalism," Speech, Osawatomie, Kansas, August 31, 1910.

MODEL, MONUMENT TO THE 122ND NY VOLUNTEER INFANTRY REGIMENT
The 122nd New York Volunteer Infantry was known as the "Onondagas," because it was raised in Onondaga County. This model is a replica of one that the State of New York dedicated on the Gettysburg Battlefield in 1888. The monument is topped by the cross that is the symbol of the Union 6th Army Corps and is fronted with a bronze of the Seal of the State of New York. *(Courtesy of the Onondaga Historical Association)*

Theodore Parker lecturing in New York

Parker was a prominent Boston Transcendentalist and one of the nation's most celebrated abolitionists. He advocated resistance to the Fugitive Slave Act and supported John Brown's raid on Harpers Ferry. His speeches would inspire Abraham Lincoln, Martin Luther King Jr., Betty Friedan, and others. *(New York State Library, Manuscripts and Special Collections)*

The exhibit featured the State Library's copy of the Proclamation, along with the State Archives' copy of the 1962 speech in which Martin Luther King Jr., spoke to the document's enduring power. People in nine New York cities—from Long Island to the North Country and from the Hudson River to the Great Lakes—lined up for as long as three hours to see documents that continue to hold strong meaning for New Yorkers and other Americans today.

As it turns out, too, "The First Step to Freedom" was a prelude to an even bigger act of remembrance: the State Museum's opening of a nearly 7,000-square-foot exhibition entitled "An Irrepressible Conflict: The Empire State in the Civil War." As shown in the pages that follow, "An Irrepressible Conflict" interprets the Civil War in its entirety—from the early nineteenth century (when New York was the largest slave state in the North), through the war years themselves (when New York State supplied more men, money, and materiel to the war effort than any other state), and up to the memory of the war today (when New York continues to reflect and influence America's memory). This is indeed an "epic story of conflict and courage,"[2] and it is indeed a story about America that New Yorkers can tell better than anyone else. For years, historians and officials in other states—particularly in the South—insisted that slavery was a benevolent institution and that the Civil War was caused by Northern aggression and fought to settle a dispute over states' rights. This was an argument that was still persuasive fifty years ago, even among some New Yorkers.

Others, however, knew differently. They understood, as New York's William H. Seward did in 1858, that the Civil War was always an "irrepressible conflict." Two different societies—one free and the other slave—could never have co-existed harmoniously. Most New Yorkers (and many others) know this now, thanks in part to social and political upheavals and lessons learned during the last fifty years. The legacy of slavery lives on in the twenty-first century, too, and it raises continuing questions about race relations, the meaning of American freedom, the proper role of government, and a whole host of other issues at the heart of the American identity.

"An Irrepressible Conflict" opened to the public for a year-and-a-half on September 22, 2012, the 150th anniversary of Lincoln's Preliminary Emancipation, and it quickly gained popularity, not only among historians and Civil War enthusiasts, but also among children learning about the war for the first time and adults learning something new about the ways in which the war and its aftermath keep teaching us lessons about ourselves. Those of us who had the privilege of bringing the exhibit to life are grateful to our friends at SUNY Press for enabling us to keep "An Irrepressible Conflict" alive for years to come through this catalogue. And we are hoping that when 2062 rolls around, some of the kids (and maybe even some of the adults) who saw the show in 2012-13 will return to the New York State Museum to see a major exhibition entitled something like "The Irrepressible Conflict Continues." It promises to be quite an event.

ROBERT WEIBLE
New York State Historian and
Chief Curator, New York State Museum

---

2. Paul Grondahl, "An epic story of conflict and courage: State Museum unveiling sweeping new exhibit on Civil War," *Albany Times-Union*, September 21, 2012.

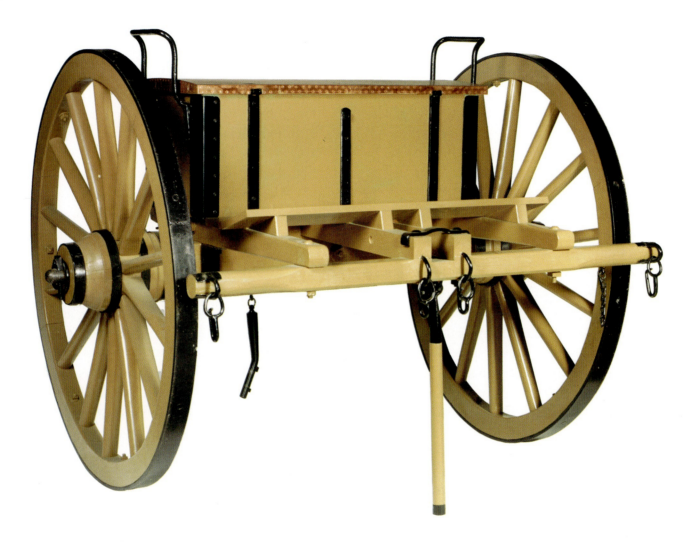

CANNON CAISSON
A restored cannon caisson—a two-wheeled cart designed to carry artillery ammunition—manufactured at the U.S. Army's Watervliet Arsenal. The Arsenal at Watervliet continues operations today and remains the U.S. Army's longest continuously operational arsenal. *(New York State Museum Collection, H-1975.75.2)*

Acknowledgments

"An Irrepressible Conflict" is an educational exhibition full of iconic artifacts, images and information that together tell a story about the Civil War. In planning "An Irrepressible Conflict," the New York State Museum reached out to other cultural institutions and individuals and asked them to help broaden the story by loaning their objects and expertise. All responded with generosity and collegiality, and as a consequence all share in the ownership of the exhibit. As always, the museum is grateful for the continuing support of the New York State Board of Regents, Commissioner of Education John King Jr., and Deputy Commissioner for Cultural Education Jeffrey Cannell. The State Museum worked in close partnership with its sister institutions in the Office of Cultural Education (OCE): the State Archives and State Library. The long list of other partners includes the following lending institutions and people: Adirondack Museum, Albany Institute of History & Art, Association of Public Historians of New York State, Warren Broderick, Town of Brookhaven, Broome County Historical Society, Philip Brown Collection, Buffalo History Museum, Brenna Buscher, Chemung County Historical Society, Cornell University, Federal Bureau of Investigation, Government Appointed Historians of Western New York, Sue Greenhagen, Jean Guthrie Collection, William F. Howard Collection, Hudson-Mohawk Industrial Gateway, Robert Keough (United States Naval Landing Party), Library of Congress, Madison County Historical Society, Elizabeth Meaders Collection, Stephanie Miller, the Myer Family, New-York Historical Society, New York State Historical Association, New York State Office of General Services (RoAnn M. Destito, Commissioner), New York State Office of Parks, Recreation and Historic Preservation, New York State Military Museum (Division of Military and Naval Affairs), National Park Service, Onondaga Historical Association, Edwin Presley Collection,

Rochester Museum & Science Center, Barbara Russell, St. Lawrence County Historical Association, Schenectady County Historical Society, John Scherer, Alan Shineman, Gerald R. Smith, Syracuse University (Special Collections Research Center), Union College (Schaeffer Library, Manuscripts and Special Collections), Robert Yott Collection, and A. Howard Young (Capital Region Civil War Roundtable).

The realization of the exhibit, "An Irrepressible Conflict," also owes tremendously to the efforts of Nancy Kelley, Jennifer A. Lemak, Aaron Noble, and Robert Weible; as well as Darcy Benton, Nick Blais, Sue Bove, Michael Carlito, Marie Culver, Kelley Ferenac, Connie Frisbee Houde, Karen Glaz, Craig Gravina, Robert Kaschack, Chris Kobuskie, Koren Lazarou, Tom Link, Steve Loughman, Nicholas Lue, Gene Mackay, Andrew Meier, Alan Noble, Riva Packard, Pete Seymour, Owen Sherwood, Jeff Stringer, Keith Swaney, Anne Tyrrell, Vicki Weiss, Tom With, and a host of others. Neither the exhibition nor this catalogue would have been possible without the efforts of our image researcher, Bridget Enderle, and museum photographer, John Yost.

Lincoln scholar Harold Holzer provided the exhibition with an authoritative introduction, and Michael Barrett, Bob Bullock, Tom Carroll, Matt George, Dan Larkin, and Bob Mulligan all loaned their special expertise to the project. OCE also expresses gratitude to the New York Council for the Humanities for making it possible to enlist the services of three distinguished scholars: Steven Jaffe, Melinda Lawson, and Amy Murrell Taylor. The three reviewed and improved exhibit scripts at various stages of completion. Working with them was a joy for everyone. Last, but certainly not least, OCE extends special thanks to Tom Brockley and RBC Wealth Management for the generous financial support that made the exhibition possible, and to James Peltz and his professional staff at SUNY Press for the patience and guidance that helped make this catalogue a reality.

1896 RECEIPT
Bromley Hoke's receipt for dues paid to Farrell Post 51, G. A. R.
(New York State Library, Manuscripts and Special Collections)

Antebellum New York

Jennifer A. Lemak

New York State led the nation in transforming society, politics, and finance. It was a place of ambitious and conflicting ideas. Once the largest slave state in the North, New York became a center for abolitionism and other reform movements. At the same time, many New Yorkers profited from their business relationships with Southern slaveholders. In the end, the differences between opponents and supporters of slavery would become an "irrepressible conflict" for New Yorkers and all Americans.

Slavery in New York

Slavery—forced labor—is a system that was central to many societies beginning in ancient times. In the sixteenth century, Europeans, African traders, and New World colonists opened the Atlantic slave trade in North, Central, and South America and the Caribbean. The Dutch West India Company settled New York in 1624 as a fur trading outpost known as New Netherland. The Dutch played a major role in the African slave trade. The first enslaved Africans arrived in New Amsterdam (later New York City) in 1626 to help build forts and roads, clear forests, and labor on farms.

When the English took control of New Netherland in 1664, there were an estimated eight hundred Africans—seventy-five of whom were probably free. The Duke of York held a large amount of stock in the Royal African Company, a powerful slave-trading corporation, and as a result, slavery in the colony rapidly expanded as the duke's representatives promoted the importation of slaves. The slave trade quickly became one of New York's most prosperous businesses. In 1698, there were 2,170 slaves in the colony; by 1750, the

SLAVE BILL OF SALE, 1796
This Mohawk Valley document records the purchase of "a negro named Cesar" in exchange for four hundred and twenty-five pounds of ginseng root.
(New York State Library, Manuscripts and Special Collections)

1

Harry from Canajoharie

In 1806, John Diefendorff and John S. Glenn, businessmen from Canajoharie, Montgomery County, posted a $50 reward for the return of their slave named Harry. Harry had run away on June 3, 1805. He was thought to be in Boston in 1808 and in 1810 was spotted in Rutland, Vermont—but his owners never found him. Underestimating Harry's resolve to be free, Glenn wrote in September 1811, "[A]lthough I bought [Harry] under price I bought him at uncertainty at my own risk."

SLAVE COLLAR, BRASS, C.1806
This collar is inscribed "J. S. Glenn/ GLENN/ Montgomery Co N.Y." Slave collars were typically used as a means to control slaves, especially those who resisted their masters. Although there is no historical proof that John Glenn required all of his slaves to wear such a collar, it is possible he had this one made in reaction to Harry's escape.
(New York State Museum Collection, H-2006.59.1)

Charlestown 20 Sep 1811

Gentlemen

I send you by My Son Jacob the
Bill of Sale I have of My Negro Slave Harry
also the power of attorney to take and appre:
hend him and bring him home. Also an
Acct of Expences I have been at Since I owned
him I had A Letter of A friend of mine in boston
that Harry was thair I Sent my Son in pur:
suit of him to Boston it was not my Slave
Jacob returned without him although I bought
of Mr Dravendorp Law and Under price I bought
him at an Uncertainty at my own risk. I
was to find him or not I had paid for him
the Sum of £45. the Expences I have been at
to get him is Rising of two Hundred Dollars
my Son will deliver you the Acct. which I
Desire to Lay before the Jury to Consider I Can
prove by Son that it is A just Acct. of Expences
I have been at Since I owned him. also the

account of going and coming home to rutland
Gentlemen by your Councill Advice the Law was in
my favour. I Could recover the price of the Negro
and costs I have been at I hope you will do your
best endeavors to recover all my the negro
and all my Damages and Costs I have been
at and the Intrest of the Money I have Laid out
So long I am Gentlemen With due respat
Gentlemen your friend and Most

Humble Servent

John S Glen

Messrs. Paine & Hall Esquires
Attorneys at Law Troy

by Jacob S. Glen

Fifty Dollars Reward.

RAN away from the subscriber, in Canajoharry, Montgomery County, on the 3d day of June, 1805, a Negro Man, named HARRY ; between five feet four and eight inches high, yellow complexion, *is about 28 years of age* has a scar across his right cheek, middling straight built, and speaks Dutch and English.   It is supposed he is in New-England. Whoever will apprehend the said Negro, and confine him in goal, either at Albany, Troy or Johnstown, shall have the above reward ; ~~or if any person will confine him in any goal, and give information to the subscriber, he shall receive *Thirty Dollars.*~~

JOHN DIEFENDORFF.

CANAJOHARY, March, 1806.

ALBANY:—PRINTED BY *ROBERT PACKARD.*

NB I will pay the above reward If any person deliver said Negro Harrey to me in Schenectady

John S Glen

REWARD BROADSIDE, 1806
Enslavement was a horrible existence, and Harry resisted slavery by running away. Other slaves fought for their freedom by attacking their masters through poison, arson, breaking tools, and even inciting riots. Punishment for these offenses was severe. *(New York State Museum Collection, H-2006.59.2)*

slave population was over 9,000—the largest number of slaves in any colony north of Maryland.

When New Yorkers debated freeing the colonies from English rule, most were unwilling to resolve the contradiction of slavery's existence in a new country based on the ideals of democracy and freedom. At the end of the eighteenth century, the census reported that 82 percent of the 25,875 black New Yorkers were still in bondage, yet change in New York State was on the horizon. In 1785, the New York Manumission Society, with John Jay as president and Alexander Hamilton as secretary, stirred up the legislature by trying to pass a gradual emancipation bill. Although the bill was rejected, the state legislature attempted to address the institution by eliminating the slave trade, eliminating a bond required of masters freeing slaves, and giving slaves some legal rights in court. By the end of the century, antislavery sentiment strengthened enough to encourage passage of a gradual emancipation law. This law stipulated that female slaves born after July 4, 1799, were freed at age twenty-five, while male slaves born after that date were freed at age twenty-eight—securing a generation of productive work years from these slaves. Finally, in 1817, a new law gave freedom to all enslaved New Yorkers, regardless of age, on July 4, 1827.

PETER BRONCK BILL OF SALE, 1762
This document records the sale and transfer of slaves held by Peter Bronck of Coxsackie, New York, to Mathew Van den Berck. It specifically notes that the sale was conducted according to the "customs of the plantation of British America," a recognition that slavery had been outlawed in England by 1762, although it was still legal in the colonies. *(New York State Library, Manuscripts and Special Collections)*

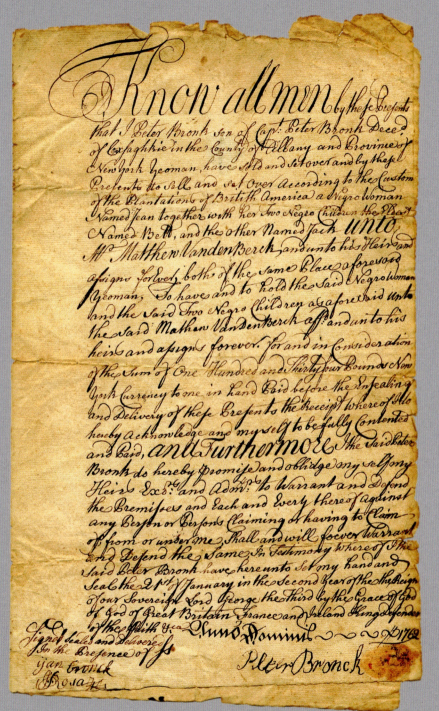

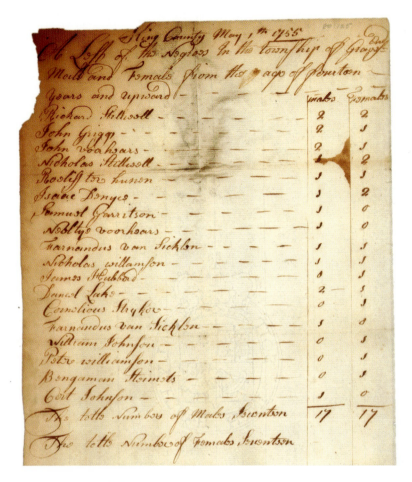

SLAVE CENSUS, KINGS COUNTY, C. 1750S

The New York Colony Council Papers, 1664–1781, included an official enumeration of slaves within each county. Slavery permeated the entire New York colony throughout the eighteenth century. Slaves in rural areas lived on small farms in groups of two to five and made up the majority of the owner's wealth. In urban areas, slaves lived with the middle and upper classes in groups of three to five. Slaves, whether rural or urban, usually lived in their owner's household and were treated as members of the extended family—making it difficult for bondsmen to have families of their own. The exceptions to this were the few large plantations in the Hudson Valley, such as Philipsburg Manor, or very wealthy urbanites who used slaves as a badge of wealth.
(New York State Archives)

EMANCIPATION RIBBON FROM WAVERLY, NEW YORK, 1901

Many emancipation celebrations did not take place in New York State until July 5, 1827. It was a contradiction for the free blacks who organized those events to celebrate freedom in a country that still allowed slavery. Emancipation celebrations took place well into the twentieth century and gave African Americans an opportunity to celebrate their communities.
(New York State Museum Collection, H-2012.12.1)

We John G. Vanderheyden, Hugh Peebles & Benja
-min Smith Executors of the Last will & Testament
of Dirck Y. Vanderheyden Esqr. late of the City of
Troy Deceased— do hereby Certify that the said Dirck
Y. in and by his said Last Will & Testament has Mana
-mitted & forever freed from Slavery his three Slaves in
the manner following viz; "I Do hereby Manu-
=mit & Discharge forever from Slavery my young
man Harry & my Female Slave Peggy & my Negro
girl Mary immediately from and after my Decease, re-
=questing & Directing the Executors of this my Last will to
take the necessary steps & measures to free & Discharge
my heirs & Estate from being liable for their mainten
-ance and Support" We the said Executors do therefore by Virtue of the said Will hereby Manumit &
forever Discharge from Slavery the said persons
above named— Dated Troy June 14. 1818.—

NB. The word & over an erasure in
the 5th line from top before execution

D. L. Wendell

Hugh Peebles.

John G. Vanderheyden

Benj. Smith

Executors of the
Last will & Testa-
t. of D.Y.D Heyden Dec

We John London and Nathan Bouton overseers of the poor of
the City of Troy in the County of Rensselaer in the State of New
York do hereby certify that we have examined Peggy Van Vranken
a Female now a late a Slave who belonged to Dirck Y. Vanderheyden
late of Troy aforesaid Deceased at the time of his Death and that
said Peggy appears to be under the age of forty five Years and of
sufficient ability to provide for herself. In Witness whereof we
have hereunto set our hands & Seals this Ninth day of April Eighteen hundred and Eighteen

John London

Nathan Bouton

CERTIFICATE OF MANUMISSION, TROY, NEW YORK, 1818
This document legally frees (or manumits) three slaves belonging to
Dirck Y. Vanderheyden of Troy, New York.
(New York State Library, Manuscripts and Special Collections)

I Sell the Shadow to Support the Substance.
SOJOURNER TRUTH.

Sojourner Truth, 1797–1883
Crusader for Abolition and Women's Rights

Sojourner Truth was born into slavery in Esopus, Ulster County. She spoke only Dutch as a child and never learned to read or write. Sold three times before the age of thirty, Truth escaped to freedom with her infant daughter in 1826—a year before emancipation. "I did not run off, for I thought that wicked," she later said, "but I walked off, believing that to be all right."

After emancipation Truth moved to New York City and worked as a housekeeper. In 1843, she began to preach about abolition and women's rights. She remained an activist for both causes until her death at eighty-six.

"He whipped her till the flesh was deeply lacerated, and the blood streamed from her wounds . . . 'what a way is this of treating human beings?'"

—*from* The Narrative of Sojourner Truth, *1850*

SOJOURNER TRUTH, PHOTO PRINT, 1864
This photo, captioned "I Sell the Shadow to Support the Substance," appeared on promotional cards for Truth and her abolitionist activities. *(New York State Library, Manuscripts and Special Collections)*

The Mob demanding that Quack be burnt.

evident absurdity, and nobody remembering that on that morning a plumber

JAMES, DUKE OF YORK
In 1664, England took control of the former Dutch colony. James,
Duke of York, had stock in the Royal African Trading Company.
(New York Public Library)

THE MOB DEMANDING THAT QUACK BE BURNT.
The image depicts the burning of a slave named Quack in
Manhattan in 1741 for participation in a slave conspiracy. Although
evidence was suspect, no lawyer would serve as his defense counsel.
(New York Public Library)

A Transportation Revolution
Setting the Stage for Modern Warfare

After the American Revolution, New Yorkers transformed their state into a national economic powerhouse and leader in modernization. Steamboats, canals, and railroads all premiered in New York State and led the North to an industrialized economy and solidified New York as a world city and international port.

Taking advantage of the natural waterway that provided access from the Atlantic Ocean to the interior of the country; Robert Fulton built the first commercial steamship in 1807. Known as the *Clermont,* it carried passengers between Albany and New York City via the Hudson River. Within a few years, steamboats were common on the Hudson River.

The next technological innovation solidified New York's place in American history. Between 1817 and 1825, the state financed and built the Erie Canal. When it opened, the 363-mile canal was an engineering marvel that cut transportation costs between the Eastern seaboard and the Great Lakes by 95 percent, lowered food costs in Eastern cities, and enabled the shipment of manufactured goods to the Midwest. Soon after the canal's opening, upstate New York became one of the world's great grain-growing regions and New York emerged as the nation's largest city and the center of international trade. In addition to transforming transportation, agriculture, and the economy in the state, the Erie Canal also attracted people—both from other states and immigrants—to New York in droves. Railroads followed in 1831 and were initially conceived to supplement the Erie Canal, but they too exploded, and by 1850 there were 1,700 miles of track with much more under construction.

New York State's population grew in the decades before the Civil War—from 1.3 million residents in 1820 to almost 4 million in 1860. Immigrants, mostly Irish and German, were lured by the prospect of work on canals, railroads, and farms and in factories and private homes. By 1860,

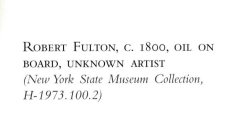

ROBERT FULTON, C. 1800, OIL ON BOARD, UNKNOWN ARTIST
(New York State Museum Collection, H-1973.100.2)

immigrants accounted for almost half of New York City's total population and many native New Yorkers feared foreigners would take their jobs and were hostile toward Catholicism. Nativists fought against foreign influences in their communities, sometimes violently, and often through political organizations, such as the American Republican Party in the 1840s and the Know-Nothing Party in the 1850s.

Once New York City was connected to the West by the Erie Canal and to Europe by its port, its primacy as the capital of American commerce and culture was guaranteed. By 1820, New York was the nation's biggest city. New York City was the nation's largest trading and manufacturing center. Cotton, more than any other product, was responsible for New York's preeminence in foreign commerce. Massive quantities of slave-grown cotton were processed by Northern textile mills and shipped from its port. Many New Yorkers profited from the cotton trade and were not eager to see slavery abolished. New York's complex and robust transportation system, which developed in the eighteenth and nineteenth centuries, tied those interested even closer to the slave South. Ironically, these same infrastructure improvements became the backbone of the advanced transportation network that enabled the Union war effort to overwhelm and defeat the Confederacy.

Clermont MODEL, 1949 (11 ½" x 8" x 39")
Robert Fulton (1765–1815) invented the first commercial steamboat, known as the *Clermont*. In 1807, the *Clermont* made history, traveling the 150-mile trip from New York City to Albany in thirty-two hours, or five miles per hour. *(New York State Museum Collection, H-1948.7.1.A-B)*

THE WEDDING OF THE WATERS (FROM COLDEN'S MEMOIR)
New York celebrated the grand achievement of the opening of the
Erie Canal with parades, speeches, and parties across the state. The
culmination of these events occurred on November 4, 1825, when
Governor Clinton dumped a keg of water from Lake Erie into
the New York Harbor, hence combining the Great Lakes with the
Atlantic Ocean. The Erie Canal was officially open for business.
(New York Public Library)

ERIE CANAL OPENING COMMEMORATION PLAQUE, MARBLE, 1825
This marble plaque was dedicated by Governor DeWitt Clinton at
Lockport, Niagara County, during the opening ceremonies of the
Erie Canal. *(New York State Museum Collection, H-1950.10.1)*

TRUNK, C.1829
The Erie Canal was a spectacular technological innovation that affected
New Yorkers' culture, religion, education, and arts. This trunk lined
with wallpaper depicts the canal at Rochester as a well-developed
urban boom town, which, at the time the trunk was made, had not
happened yet. Most popular views of the Erie Canal portrayed the area
as a bucolic rural wilderness. Also interesting is that someone thought
there would be enough of a market to mass produce wallpaper with
the view of the Erie Canal at the Rochester aqueduct.
(New York State Museum Collection, H-1988.79.12)

STAFFORDSHIRE PITCHER, ENGLAND, 1825, *above*
Staffordshire plates, platters, and pitchers decorated with views
from the Erie Canal were popular keepsake items. This pitcher
commemorates the opening of the Erie Canal at Utica, New York.
(New York State Museum Collection, H-1976.199.3)

**GRAND CANAL CELEBRATION MEDAL AND ORIGINAL BOX, PEWTER,
BIRD'S-EYE MAPLE, PAPER, 1826,** *below*
The City of New York commissioned a commemorative medal
for dignitaries involved with the canal's celebration. Cabinetmaker
Duncan Phyfe made the medal's boxes out of wood from western
forests, which traveled east in the first canal boat, the *Seneca Chief.*
(New York State Museum Collection, H-1949.8.1, A-B)

LOCKPORT
(New York State Museum Collection, H-1969.9.2)

"New York is greater than Paris or Constantinople, and will evidently be hereafter greater than London."
—*Putnam's Monthly, March 1855*

CANAL BOATS ON THE NORTH RIVER, NEW YORK IN *Gleason's Pictorial Drawing Room Companion.*
(New York State Library, Manuscripts and Special Collections)

MAP OF THE RAILROADS OF THE STATE OF NEW YORK, C. 1861

Railroads—which were first built to supplement canals—eventually came to dominate New York's transportation systems. In 1831, the state incorporated the first railroad company—the Mohawk and Hudson—connecting Albany and Schenectady with sixteen miles of track. A fury of railroad building followed; by 1850 more than thirty railroads served the state with over 1,600 miles of track and another 1,000 under construction. By the Civil War, New York had the nation's most extensive railroad system. *(New York State Library, Manuscripts and Special Collections)*

Agriculture and the Erie Canal

Farming in New York changed dramatically after the Erie Canal opened. Previously, farmers grew crops principally for subsistence. Afterward, many sold their goods at commercial markets. By 1860, New York State was the nation's leading producer of dairy products, potatoes, hops, flax, and lumber. At the same time, the state was a main supplier of cattle, wool, wheat, and other grains. Crops could be shipped easily via the canal and railroad to markets all over the world.

GRAIN SCOOP, C. 1850 *(above)*
FLOUR BARREL, C. 1840 *(below)*
Several types of grains were shipped from the Midwest through Buffalo, and east along the Erie Canal. Barrels such as this one were probably used to transport flour along the canal.
(New York State Museum Collection, H-1990.103.1 and H-1969.66.142)

STARBUCK TROJAN PLOW, 1850
This handsomely decorated plow was manufactured in Troy, New York. According to the records of the New York State Agricultural Society, this plow placed fifth at the plow trials held in Albany in 1850. *(New York State Museum Collection, H-1901.1.21)*

17

Wholesale Store !
No. 25 JAMES STREET,
DIRECTLY OPPOSITE STANWIX HALL,
ROME, N. Y.

45

We have just returned from New York, and are now receiving large additions to our former Stock, and believe we can offer Bargains inferior to none in CENTRAL NEW YORK. We are determined to give the Purchaser

THE BEST OF GOODS
AT THE VERY LOWEST POSSIBLE PRICES.

Our Stock is equal to many City Jobbing Houses, and Prices will be found to compare with New York City, adding difference of transportation. It consists in part of

70 hhds. Sugar, Molasses and Syrups,	50 qtls. Cod Fish,	
100 bbls. " " " em-	800 bbls. ex. Genesee and com. brand Flour,	
bracing every variety,	400 " coarse and fine Salt,	
80 packages every style Teas,	500 bags Dairy Salt,	
75 bags Coffee, all qualities,	75 doz. Bed Cords,	Manufacturer's Prices,
75 boxes, kegs and frails of Raisins,	40 coils Rope,	
40 " Sperm and Mould Candles,	20 doz. Brooms,	
40 " Herring,	200 cans Mustard,	
75 " Hard Soap,	100 gross Gates' Matches, at Manufacturer's Prices,	
300 " Dunbarton Window Glass, at factory prices,	25 boxes Starch,	
	100 lbs. Bar Lead,	
40 " Pipes,	4000 lbs. Saleratus,	
30 " Tobacco,	1 bbl. Clover,	
15 jars Black Snuff,	1 " Nutmegs,	
40 bladders Scotch Do.,	500 Seamless Bags,	
40 pkges. Mackerel,	20 doz. Patent Pails,	

And many other Articles, of which we have a large supply, such as Pork, Water Lime, Lamp Oil, Cassia, Currants, Citron, Seedless Raisins, Pepper, Spice; Castile, Toilet and Erasive Soaps; Maccaroni, Tapioca, Alum, Epsom Salts, Shot; Foolscap, Letter and Wrapping Paper; Wick and Twine, Almonds, Filberts, Brazil and English Walnuts, Camphor, Gum, Cream Tartar, Soda, Putty, Cigars, Bird Seed, Tubs, Boxes, &c., &c.

We have also a good Assortment of Pocket and Table Cutlery and Shelf Hardware generally, Broom and Linen Twine in great variety, Mill and Cross-cut Saws, Wood and Earthen Ware, &c., &c. We have made arrangement with the Manufactory to be supplied with Nails of a superior quality, all hot cut; and are prepared to fill orders for any amount as cheap as can be done any where in the State, adding transportation, &c., to this Place.

Orders from Merchants and others solicited, which we will endeavor to attend to punctually, and fill satisfactorily, and at Prices as low as if they or their Agent were in our Store. When in Town call and examine our Stock and Prices.

Goods purchased of us will be delivered at the Rail Road Depot, or shipped on board Canal Boats, free of charge.

BLOSS & FOOT,
ROME.

SEPT. 15, 1852.

A. Sandford & Co, Printers, Citizen Office, Rome.

BROADSIDE, ROME, ONEIDA COUNTY, 1852
Rome, New York was a popular stop on the Erie Canal to purchase provisions. This broadside advertises new items available for sale at the Bloss & Foot Wholesale Store.
(New York State Library, Manuscripts and Special Collections)

TRUNK, C. 1850
This trunk was used by Dorothea Ammon when she immigrated from Colberg Larhsen-Neiningen, Germany, to Albany, Albany County, in the 1850s. With the immigrant population increasing in New York State, so too did their political power. Most immigrants leaned toward the pro-slavery wing of the Democratic Party, because they feared competition with free blacks in the workplace.
(New York State Museum Collection, H-1986.58.1)

CHOICE
AND
Valuable Lands.

THE undersigned and their associates, having become proprietors of all the land belonging to the Holland Land Company, on and adjacent to the ERIE CANAL, which remained unsold, in the counties of Genesee, Orleans, Erie, and Niagara, and contained in the following townships, to wit:

No. 13 and 14	in Range 1,
" 13 and 14	" 2,
" 13 and 14	" 3,
" 13 and 14	" 4,
" 13	" 5,
" 13, 14, and 15	" 6,
" 12, 13, and 14	" 7,
" 12, 13, and 15	" 8,

offer the same for sale at reduced prices, either by townships, or in quantities to suit purchasers.

No tract of land in the State of New-York can offer greater inducements to agriculturists than the foregoing. It is situated in the most flourishing section of the state, interspersed with industrious settlers, with a soil not surpassed by any in the country for fertility, and mostly covered with valuable timber of various kinds: superadded to which advantages, the facilities to market by *Canal Navigation*, place these lands on an equality with any in the United States. A portion of them are well adapted for the growth of hemp, which article must in time become one of the staple productions of this state.

Offices are kept at Batavia and at Albany. The terms of sale to companies, or to individual settlers, will be very favorable, and the most unquestionable title given to those who purchase.

TRUMBULL CARY, *of Batavia.*
RUSSEL FORSYTH,
WILLIAM L. MARCY, } *of Albany.*
BENJAMIN KNOWER,
CHARLES E. DUDLEY,
THOMAS HILLHOUSE, *of Watervliet.*

Albany, State of New-York, March, 1828.

Packard & Van Benthuysen, Printers, 435 South Market-street, Albany.

ANTELBELLUM COTTON DRESS
Ties between New York textile manufacturers and the Southern cotton economy extended well into upstate. Finished products, like this child's dress, were manufactured from imported southern cotton by New York textile manufacturers. Both cotton merchants and textile manufacturers made massive amounts of money from southern cotton. *(New York State Museum Collection, H-1947.1.35)*

BROADSIDE, CHOICE AND VALUABLE LANDS, 1828
An 1828 advertisement for land along the Erie Canal.
(New York State Library, Manuscripts and Special Collections)

An Age of Reform

The Erie Canal's success put the Empire State on the cutting edge of reform at a time when Americans were searching for their young nation's identity and purpose. New Yorkers felt called upon—not just to better their own lives—but to perfect society. Many worked to improve public institutions. Some, unsettled by change, sought comfort in religion, while still others became evangelical crusaders determined to cure the country of its social and political ills.

The Second Great Awakening was a Christian revival movement in the first half of the nineteenth century. Upstate New York—the Erie Canal corridor, in particular—was a hotbed of religious activity. Disrupted by rapid social and economic change before the Civil War, the area was fertile ground for the spread of evangelical Protestantism and reform movements dedicated to abolition, temperance, public education, and women's rights.

Abolition

New Yorkers did away with slavery in their state in 1827—and afterward led the movement to abolish it elsewhere in their country. Religiously motivated abolitionists and many free blacks believed that all men were created equal and that slavery was a moral abomination that could not be tolerated in a free country. However, they constituted only a minority of New York's population. Many other New Yorkers were indifferent or resistant to the notion of racial equality, but they still opposed slavery. They favored the principle of free labor, especially in the territories—where they hoped to expand railroads and build Northern-styled businesses and farms.

Abolition societies sought converts through lectures, sermons, conventions, pamphlets, newspapers, and broadsides—all depicting the evils of slavery. Societies were highly concentrated in New York State, especially upstate and among free black communities.

The American Anti-Slavery Society (AASS) was founded in 1833 by William Lloyd Garrison and New York City merchants Arthur and Lewis Tappan. The AASS sought to abolish slavery peacefully. By 1836, New York State had 103 local auxiliaries of the AASS—20 percent of the nation's total.

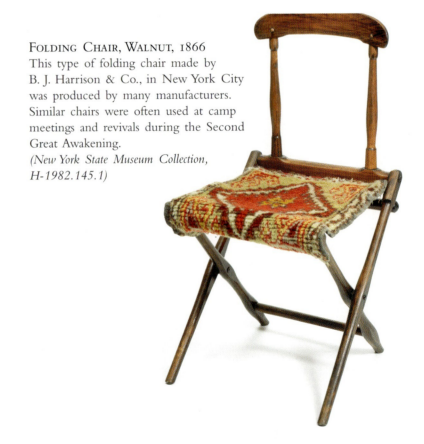

FOLDING CHAIR, WALNUT, 1866
This type of folding chair made by B. J. Harrison & Co., in New York City was produced by many manufacturers. Similar chairs were often used at camp meetings and revivals during the Second Great Awakening.
(New York State Museum Collection, H-1982.145.1)

METHODIST CAMP MEETING, PRINT, 1836
Social and religious excitement was so intense in western New York that the area would eventually come to be known as the "Burned-over District." It was so named, because the frequency of religious revivals left the area with no one left to convert or *burn. (New York State Museum Collection, H-1976.26.13)*

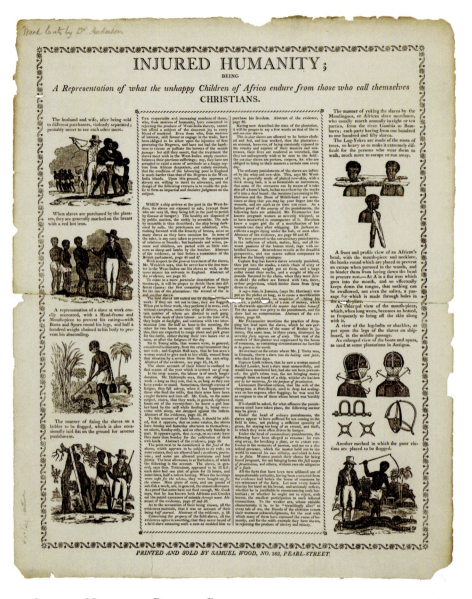

The Slave Auction, by John Rogers, painted plaster, 1859
John Rogers created this sculpture of a slave family being ripped apart at an auction shortly before the Civil War began. Rogers was praised by abolitionists and vilified by Southerners for creating a sculpture based on the subject of a slave auction. *(Albany Institute of History & Art)*

Injured Humanity; Being a Representation of what the unhappy Children of Africa endure from those who call themselves Christians, broadside, 1805
This broadside depicts the terrible conditions of slavery and the slave trade in the West Indies. Samuel Wood, a prolific Quaker-reformist publisher, printed and sold the broadside out of his office at 362 Pearl Street in New York. *(New York State Library, Manuscripts and Special Collections)*

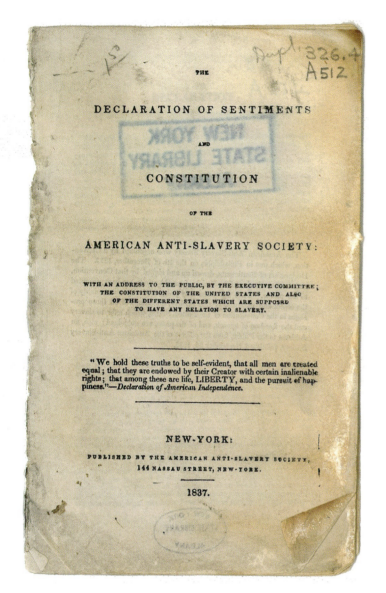

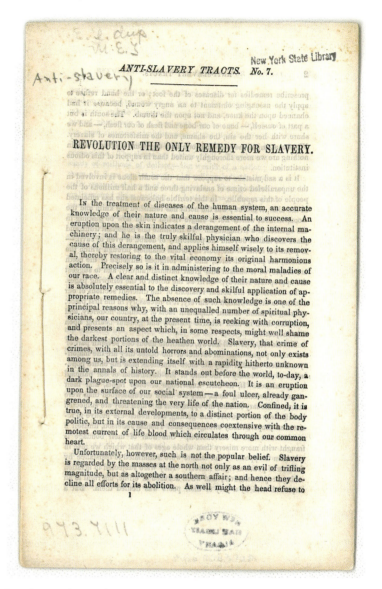

The Declaration of Sentiments and Constitution of the American Anti-Slavery Society, 1837
By the time this pamphlet was published, the American Anti-Slavery Society had 1,350 local chapters with around 250,000 members. *(New York State Library, Manuscripts and Special Collections)*

Revolution the Only Remedy for Slavery, published by the American Anti-Slavery Society, 1855
Frederick Douglass and William Wells Brown, both escaped slaves, were leaders within the American Anti-Slavery Society. The society's headquarters were located in New York City. *(New York State Library, Manuscripts and Special Collections)*

THE

ANTI-SLAVERY

ALPHABET.

IN THE MORNING SOW THY SEED.

PHILADELPHIA:
PRINTED FOR THE ANTI-SLAVERY FAIR.
1847.

Merrihew & Thompson, Printers.

THE

ANTI-SLAVERY

ALPHABET.

"In the morning sow thy seed."

PHILADELPHIA:
PRINTED FOR THE ANTI-SLAVERY FAIR.
1847.

Merrihew & Thompson, Printers, 7 Carter's alley.

TO OUR LITTLE READERS.

Listen, little children, all,
Listen to our earnest call:
You are very young, 'tis true,
But there's much that you can do,
Even you can plead with men
That they buy not slaves again,
And that those they have may be
Quickly set at liberty.
They may hearken what you say,
Though from us they turn away.
Sometimes, when from school you walk,
You can with your playmates talk,
Tell them of the slave child's fate,
Motherless and desolate.
And you can refuse to take
Candy, sweetmeat, pie or cake,
Saying "no"—unless 'tis free—
"The slave shall not work for me."
Thus, dear little children, each
May some useful lesson teach;
Thus each one may help to free
This fair land from slavery.

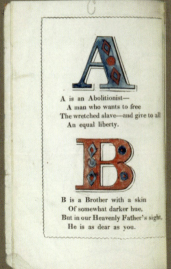

A is an Abolitionist—
A man who wants to free
The wretched slave—and give to all
An equal liberty.

B is a Brother with a skin
Of somewhat darker hue,
But in our Heavenly Father's sight,
He is as dear as you.

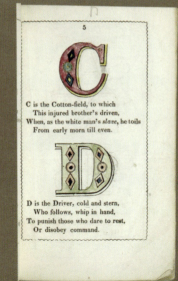

C is the Cotton-field, to which
This injured brother's driven,
When, as the white man's *slave*, he toils
From early morn till even.

D is the Driver, cold and stern,
Who follows, whip in hand,
To punish those who dare to rest,
Or disobey command.

E is the Eagle, soaring high;
An emblem of the free;
But while we chain our brother man,
Our type he cannot be.

F is the heart-sick Fugitive,
The slave who runs away,
And travels through the dreary night,
But hides himself by day.

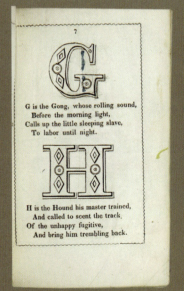

G is the Gong, whose rolling sound,
Before the morning light,
Calls up the little sleeping slave,
To labor until night.

H is the Hound his master trained,
And called to scent the track,
Of the unhappy fugitive,
And bring him trembling back.

THE ANTI-SLAVERY ALPHABET, 1847, Abolitionists taught children about the horrors of slavery.
(New York State Library, Manuscripts and Special Collections)

Pro-Slavery in New York State

New Yorkers were divided over the slavery issue. Some Northerners simply feared change and worried that forcing an end to slavery would split the nation and disrupt its economy. Others, especially in downstate communities, more actively supported slavery and good relations with Southerners. Pro-slavery advocates included businessmen engaged in the cotton trade and working-class immigrants who worried that newly emancipated slaves might compete for their jobs. Pro-slavery mobs backed by "gentlemen of property and standing" would often resort to violence in protest of abolitionist meetings.

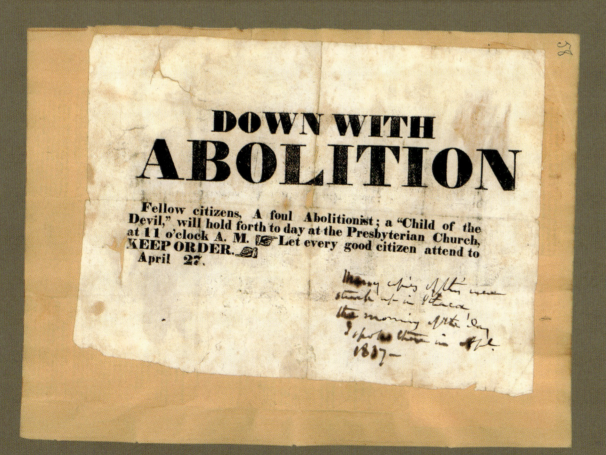

DOWN WITH ABOLITION

Fellow citizens, A foul Abolitionist; a "Child of the Devil," will hold forth to day at the Presbyterian Church, at 11 o'clock A. M. ☞ Let every good citizen attend to KEEP ORDER. ✑
April 27.

DOWN WITH ABOLITION, BROADSIDE, 1837
This broadside was posted in Ithaca, Tompkins County, when Gerrit Smith visited to speak about abolition.
(Courtesy of Syracuse University)

"This Fourth of July is yours, not mine. You may rejoice, I must mourn. To drag a man in fetters into the grand illuminated temple of liberty, and call upon him to join you in joyous anthems, were inhuman mockery and sacrilegious irony."

—*Frederick Douglass, Rochester 1852*

Frederick Douglass, 1818–1895

Abolitionist, Orator, Writer, and Statesman

Frederick Douglass was one of the great human rights leaders of the nineteenth century. Born into slavery in Maryland in 1818, Douglass escaped to freedom in New York City in 1838. Immersing himself in the antislavery debate, he became a leading abolitionist who gained prominence on the 1840s lecture circuit.

In 1847, Douglass moved to Rochester, where he began publishing the *North Star,* an abolitionist newspaper that circulated throughout the nation. In the 1850s, Douglass abandoned his moderate views on abolition and made such thunderous statements as, "It is not light we need, but fire. . . . We need a storm, the whirlwind, and the earthquake."

Frederick Douglass, full plate daguerreotype, c.1845, *left*
This daguerreotype was taken by an unknown photographer around 1845 and may be the earliest image of Frederick Douglass.
(Onondaga Historical Association)

Letter from Frederick Douglass to Hannah Fuller, 1855/1857
This is one of six letters written by Frederick Douglass to Miss Hannah Fuller, organizer of the Skaneateles Ladies Anti-Slavery Society. Written between 1855 and 1857, the letters show the close working relationships that Douglass forged with white women leaders of the antislavery movement. It is clear from the letters that Douglass was an ardent proponent of women's rights and recognized the contributions women made to the antislavery movement.
(New York State Library, Manuscripts and Special Collections)

Gerrit Smith, 1797–1874
Abolitionist, Philanthropist, Social Reformer

A native of Utica, Gerrit Smith was one of the state's largest land-owners in antebellum New York. Following a religious awakening in 1826, Smith devoted himself to abolition and other reform movements. He hosted the 1835 organizing convention of the New York State Anti-Slavery Society at his home in Peterboro, Madison County, supported a school for both black and white abolitionists (the Oneida Institute), and funded the 1850 Cazenovia Fugitive Slave Convention. He also backed fugitive slave rescues, the free-state cause in "Bleeding Kansas," John Brown's raid on Harpers Ferry, and the organization of the antislavery Liberty Party.

GERRIT SMITH, DAGUERREOTYPE, C.1840
Gerrit Smith was a presidential candidate on the Liberty Party ticket in 1848, 1856, and 1860. *(Peterboro Area Museum)*

GERRIT SMITH, BY DANIEL HUNTINGTON, OIL ON CANVAS, 1874
(Madison County Historical Society)

BLACK FARMERS IN
NORTH ELBA,
ESSEX COUNTY
(Adirondack Museum)

Timbuctoo: Gerrit Smith's Experiment

From 1846 through 1853, Gerrit Smith developed a plan to give away 120,000 acres of Essex and Franklin County farmland to three thousand free black men. He hoped to qualify the men to vote. Although Smith's supporters promoted the project in churches and conventions, the plan eventually failed due to poor soil, harsh Adirondack winters, and the inexperience of the farmers themselves. Black men would not get full voting rights in New York until the ratification of the Fifteenth Amendment in 1870. Timbuctoo is remembered today because the project attracted radical abolitionist John Brown and his family to a tract of land in North Elba (Essex County). Brown purchased the land in 1849 from Smith for one dollar.

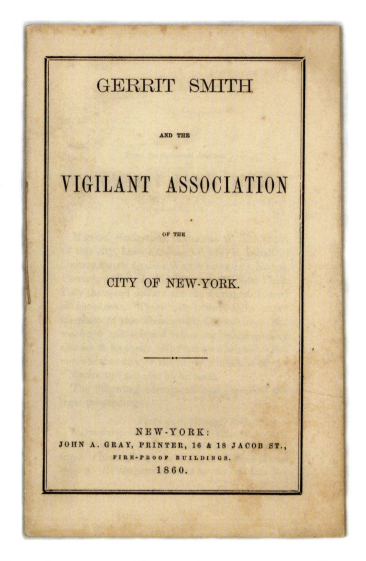

REWARD BROADSIDE, 1839

Harriet Powell's escape from slavery in October 1839 helped establish Onondaga County's national reputation as a center of abolition. Powell had accompanied her wealthy Mississippi owners to Syracuse and was persuaded by local abolitionists to run away. New York's antislavery community—including Gerrit Smith—rallied to Powell's aid and enabled her escape to Canada. Smith's cousin, women's rights pioneer Elizabeth Cady Stanton, met Powell in Peterboro and later said this was the moment when she became an "earnest abolitionist." After Powell was safe, Gerrit Smith stirred up Southern animosity—and demands for a stronger fugitive slave law—by publicly acknowledging his role in Powell's escape. Harriet Powell, he reported, was "now a free woman, safe under the shadow of the British throne."

(Onondaga Historical Association)

GERRIT SMITH AND THE VIGILANT ASSOCIATION OF THE CITY OF NEW YORK, PAMPHLET, 1860

Ardent abolitionist Gerrit Smith published this booklet in an effort to refute accusations of involvement in John Brown's raid on Harpers Ferry. Included in this booklet is a reprinting of Smith's "Address to the Slaves," given at the New York State Liberty Party Convention in Peterboro in 1842, expressing why slavery should be abolished.

(Peterboro Area Museum)

CHAIR OWNED BY PETER SMITH
At age twenty-one, Gerrit Smith took over his father's business and became one of the state's largest landowners. Peter Smith, Gerrit's father, had amassed a huge fortune as a land speculator and fur trader in the Adirondack region. Just a portion of these lands were used in the Timbuctoo experiment. (*Madison County Historical Society*)

THE CRIME OF THE ABOLITIONISTS, BOOKLET, 1862
This speech by Gerrit Smith, originally given in 1835, was reprinted and widely distributed in October 1862, possibly because by then the Civil War was in progress and abolitionists were being blamed for the war. Another possible reason for the publication of this booklet is that two weeks prior to its distribution, President Lincoln presented the Preliminary Emancipation Proclamation to his cabinet. (*Peterboro Area Museum*)

Freedom's Cause

The Cazenovia Convention

The Cazenovia Convention was the nation's largest meeting organized in protest of the federal Fugitive Slave Law (part of the Compromise of 1850). This law outraged abolitionists and free blacks everywhere by prohibiting anyone from harboring escaped slaves and requiring public officials to return runaways to their owners. Gerrit Smith organized the meeting held on August 22, 1850, in Cazenovia, Madison County. It was attended by more than two thousand people, including Frederick Douglass and fifty fugitives. Opponents of abolition were infuriated. The *Buffalo Morning Express* called Gerrit Smith a "madman and a knave."

LETTER BY CHARLES T. TORRY, 1843, *left*
This letter addressed to Charles T. Torry is from an unidentified author from New Rochelle, Westchester County. The content of the letter concerns the plight of a runaway slave from Virginia, named John Freeman. The author relays advice "that John ought to set his face towards Canada" and mentions there is someone living in Albany who would "cheerfully render him all the assistance he might need." Furthermore, the author writes, "we have collected a few dollars for him, but it is hard work to raise money for runaway slaves in this place."
(New York State Library, Manuscripts and Special Collections)

CAZENOVIA CONVENTION, DAGUERREOTYPE, *right*
Among the attendees at the Cazenovia Convention were Frederick Douglass (seated at right end of the table), Gerrit Smith (standing next to Douglass), Mary and Emily Edmonson, Theodosia Gilbert, Joseph Hathaway, George W. Clark, Samuel J. May, Charles B. Ray, and James Caleb Jackson. *(Madison County Historical Society)*

Albany Anti-Slavery Office,

No. 10 LARK STREET, ARBOR HILL.

CIRCULAR TO THE FRIENDS OF FREEDOM:

The hundreds of fugitives that have fallen to my care during the last twelve years, have required a great deal of labor and expense to make them comfortable. They are sent to me by the Underground Railroad, south of Albany, and in many cases they come poorly clad and greatly in want of clothes, such as coats, pants and under garments, both males and females. Whatever is sent, clothing or money, shall be faithfully used for that purpose. We have received some articles of clothing and money in this city, and from abroad, from ladies and gentlemen, for which they have our thanks. We devote all our time to the care of the oppressed who come among us; our pay is small, but yet we are willing to continue to do what we can for them. From the 1st of November, 1857, to April 1st, 1858, the number of fugitives which passed through Albany, was 121. Paid $2 for passage each, amounting to $242. We have arrivals every few days from Southern oppression; we forward them to the next depot, and from there they are forwarded to Canada. If any information is wanted concerning how many come through from time to time, they can address a line to the Albany papers.

All letters or packages must be directed to S. MYERS, or to the Anti-Slavery Office, Albany. Any articles of wearing apparel can be sent by express. A general report will be given through the Albany papers every six months. My books and accounts can be inspected by the friends of the cause, at any time they wish to see them. Those that arrive at this time of the year are in want of warm clothes, especially the children. If there should be any farmers wanting help, either men or women, in the house, they can be accomodated by sending to this Office. We consider it safe for them to go into the country, and it saves expense. We have sent quite a number in the country during this season and the last, and they write to us they make good help.

P. S. Ladies and Gentlemen will please, when they receive these circulars, to send them to their friends, for we are in want of material aid.

S. MYERS,
Superintendent Underground Railroad.

Report of S. MYERS, Superintendent of the Underground Railroad:

MONEY RECEIVED by S. MYERS. By subscriptions and by Agents, $206.34. From the 1st November, 1857, up to April 1st, 1858, we have not received enough to meet the necessary expenses of the Underground Railroad. We make an appeal again to the friends of freedom to be generous towards aiding those destitute fugitives from slavery.

——— is duly authorized to collect funds for the Underground R. R. He forwards all subscriptions faithfully to this office.

From Our Own Correspondent.

[From the New-York Tribune.]

ALBANY, March 29, 1858.

Eight passengers, per Underground Railroad passed through this city during the last week, in the direction of the North Star. Why don't somebody call the attention of Mr. Stephens, or Mr. Toombs, or "Extra Billy" Smith to this incendiary? The North Star is clearly unconstitutional; as decidedly so as the Dismal Swamp or any other device which tends to lessen the value by decreasing the security of a peculiar species of property. If the President has not the power to remove this troublesome meddler with vested rights, he should make up a cause and take it before the Supreme Court, where he would find no difficulty in obtaining a decree to "put out that light" or to remove it to a Southern point or to prevent it shining, except on cloudy nights, when it can't be seen. Either would answer the purpose. I have carefully examined the Constitution of the United States and the Resolutions of '98, and can find no warrant in either for this Northern aggression. Mr Myers, the efficient agent of the Road, reports a remarkably prosperous business for this season, so far.

☞ Persons receiving this Report will please give notice to this office.

From April 1st the annual report of S. Myers, Sup't of the Underground Railroad, up to 15th February, 1859, to the committee of Gentlemen of this city. The number passed through from Southern Bondage in the last ten months has been more than any previous length of time, and they come needy as usual and by no effort of ours and when here they must be provided for, and they are the poorest of God's poor. Two hundred and sixty three have passed through my hands, for passages and other expenses, amounting to just four hundred and ninety-seven dollars, which I have received by collection in the city and from friends living out of the city. Those of our friends living out of the city have our thanks in behalf of the Bleeding Slave, for money sent by mail. Rev. Henry A. Sizer, is duly authorized as one of our agents for the Underground Depot, he has our thanks for money sent from time to time. The labors of the Rev. Henry A. Sizer will be long appreciated by the panting slave. All the moneys that I have received have been faithfully applied for the purposes specified, I am under the necessity to make an appeal for material aid to the friends of freedom, as still they come.

STEPHEN MYERS, Superintendent of the Underground R. R., 1859.

P. S. The Albany papers publish nearly every month those that pass through, I presume the friends abroad read the Albany papers.

A NORTHERN FREEMAN ENSLAVED BY NORTHERN HANDS.

Nov. 20, 1836, (Sunday,) Peter John Lee, a free colored man of Westchester Co., N. Y., was kidnapped by Tobias Boudinot, E. K. Waddy, John Lyon, and Daniel D. Nash, of N. Y., city, and hurried away from his wife and children into slavery. One went up to shake hands with him, while the others were ready to use the gag and chain. See Emancipator, March 16, and May 4, 1837. This is not a rare case.

ENGRAVING OF FREE BLACKS BEING KIDNAPPED BY BOUNTY HUNTERS IN NEW YORK
It was illegal to help a fugitive slave escape. Pro-slavery advocates in New York opposed the Underground Railroad and even helped return fugitive slaves to the South. *(New-York Historical Society)*

BROADSIDE, ALBANY, 1858, *left*
In this broadside, Stephen A. Myers requests assistance (money and clothing) to aid escaped slaves traveling through Albany to Canada. Myers signs the broadside as Superintendent of the Underground Railroad. *(New York State Library, Manuscripts and Special Collections)*

The Underground Railroad

Abolitionists organized the Underground Railroad to help runaway slaves escape to freedom. "Conductors," both black and white, often took extraordinary risks by providing fugitives with shelter, transportation, and even jobs. As many as 1,500 former slaves traveled north each year during the decades before the Civil War.

Underground Railroad routes through New York State were crucial because of the state's lengthy border with Canada and its well-developed system of canals, rivers, roads, and railroads. While thousands of escaped slaves passed through the state en route to freedom in Canada, many chose to stay in New York.

Harriet Tubman, 1820–1913
Fugitive Slave, Civil War Nurse, Suffragist, and Civil Rights Activist

Harriet Tubman was perhaps the Underground Railroad's most famous "conductor." Born a slave in Maryland, she escaped to Canada in 1849. Tubman returned to Maryland several times, leading slaves through Quaker settlements in Pennsylvania and north to New York. Her "passengers" found refuge at Gerrit Smith's home in Peterboro, Jeremy Loguen's home in Syracuse, and several places in Rochester. She also supported John Brown's raid on Harpers Ferry.

In 1859, Tubman became a New Yorker when U.S. Senator William Seward sold her a plot of land in Auburn, Cayuga County. She went on to serve as a nurse, spy, and military leader during the Civil War and afterward as a civil rights and woman's suffrage activist.

HARRIET TUBMAN, NURSE, SPY, AND SCOUT
Harriet Tubman participated in the rescue of Charles Nalle, a fugitive slave who lived in Troy, Rensselaer County, and was captured in April 1860. Hundreds of people, including Tubman, rushed to the site where Nalle was held. A riot ensued, allowing him to escape across the Hudson to West Troy and ultimately to freedom. *(Library of Congress)*

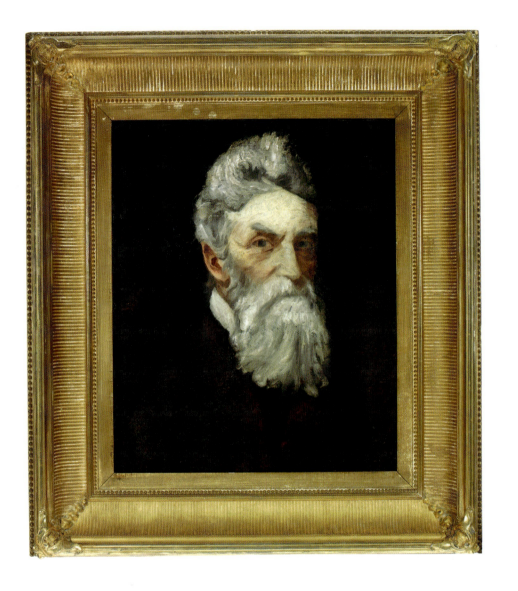

JOHN BROWN, BY SIDNEY H. MORSE (1832–1903)
Oil on ticking fabric, no date
(*New York State Office of Parks, Recreation and Historic Preservation*)

John Brown, 1800–1859

Martyr or Murderer?

John Brown is one of the most controversial figures in American history. His uncompromising hatred of slavery made him a great hero to some, but his willingness to spill blood made him an archvillain to others.

After fighting bloody battles against pro-slavery forces in Kansas in 1855, Brown found a lasting place in history when he and his followers attacked the federal arsenal at Harpers Ferry, Virginia, in 1859. They were attempting to incite a slave rebellion but were soon overpowered by militiamen and then arrested, tried, and convicted of treason. Brown was hanged on December 2, 1859, and his body was buried at his North Elba farm. To many, Brown's raid signaled the inevitability of the coming civil war.

BROWN FARM IN NORTH ELBA, ESSEX COUNTY
(*New York State Office of Parks, Recreation and Historic Preservation*)

PIECE OF ROPE, 1859
This piece of rope was used to lower John Brown into the grave.
(New York State Library, Manuscripts and Special Collections)

MORTALITY SCHEDULE FOR ESSEX COUNTY, 1860
This particular page records the death of John Brown and his son by hanging in October 1859, the month of his raid on the Harpers Ferry Federal Arsenal. However, Brown was not hanged until December 2, 1859 in Charles Town, Virginia. Shortly after, his body was sent to his home in North Elba, New York (Essex County) where it was buried. Brown's two sons, Watson and Oliver, were also killed at Harpers Ferry. Both were interred in North Elba at a later date.
(New York State Library, Manuscripts and Special Collections)

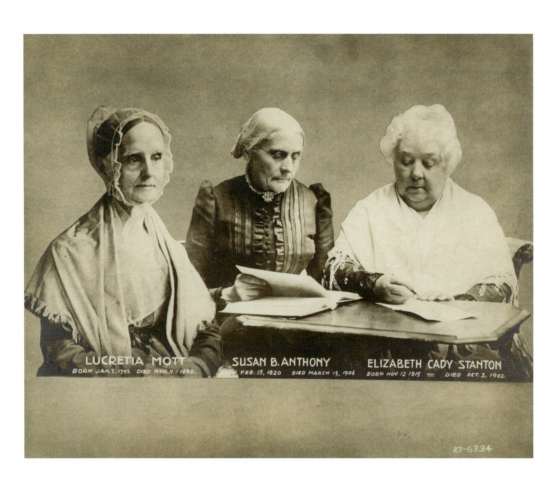

LUCRETIA MOTT; SUSAN B. ANTHONY; ELIZABETH CADY STANTON
(New York Public Library)

Women's Suffrage and Abolition

The same evangelical spirit that gave rise to the abolitionist movement also energized the women's rights movement. Abolitionism and women's rights were entwined causes for many women who empathized with the plight of slaves. Across New York, women suffragists raised money, clothed and fed fugitives, and organized their own abolition societies. The women's rights movement gained prominence when abolitionists Elizabeth Cady Stanton and Lucretia Mott organized the 1848 women's rights convention in Seneca Falls, Seneca County. The meeting attracted three hundred people and produced the Declaration of Sentiments. Frederick Douglass, who attended the meeting, described this document as "the grand basis for attaining the civil, social, political, and religious rights of women."

Antebellum Politics

The Turbulent 1850s

The 1850s was a chaotic period in New York State politics. New Yorkers were at odds over slavery, immigration, temperance, and more. Previously the Democratic and Whig parties dominated the state, but the two-party system collapsed as the debate over slavery intensified. By the end of the decade, the Democratic Party was transformed, the Whig Party had disappeared, and the Republican Party was emerging as a new force on the political scene.

CAMPAIGN TORCH, C.1860
(New York State Museum Collection, H-1974.191.35)

GRAND PROCESSION
Harper's Weekly, Oct 3, 1860 *(New York State Library)*

The Expansion of Slavery

Following the enactment of the Fugitive Slave Law in 1850, two federal actions tore the country even farther apart. The 1854 Kansas-Nebraska Act invited bloodshed by disabling the Missouri Compromise and allowing settlers in the Western Territories to determine for themselves whether or not to legalize slavery. The Supreme Court's 1857 Dred Scott decision shocked Northerners by ruling that people of African descent could not be considered citizens and, hence, had no legal rights. In effect, this eliminated the Congressional prohibition of slavery in U.S. territories. New Yorkers were appalled—not just because they tended to oppose slavery, but because they overwhelmingly supported free labor in the territories. Senator William H. Seward led the charge opposing slavery for the State of New York.

To The Independent Electors of the Town of Argyle, broadside, 1855
This broadside announces a meeting of the Whig electors of the town of Argyle, Washington County, to discuss slavery, the Missouri Compromise, and the Know-Nothing Party.
(New York State Library, Manuscripts and Special Collections)

Map of U.S. Showing Areas of Freedom and Slavery, 1856
(New York State Library, Manuscripts and Special Collections)
far right

TO THE INDEPENDENT ELECTORS OF THE
Town of Argyle.

At a meeting of the Whig Electors of the town of Argyle, held at the house of Joseph Rouse, on the 20th day of March, 1855, Wm. D. Robertson was chosen Chairman, and Ebenezer Campbell, Secretary. On motion of Wm. Boyd, the following resolutions were unanimously adopted:

RESOLVED, That to every American citizen, the right of opinion, political and religious, and also the right to openly express the same, is amply guaranteed by the Constitution and laws of his country.

RESOLVED, That we regard this right of inestimable value, for no people could be FREE who did not possess it.

RESOLVED, That we are opposed to all SECRET POLITICAL SOCIETIES, because they are incompatible with the genius and principles of Free Institutions; because they bind the members by obligations fettering an independent exercise of judgment; because they are Jesuitical in character, and demoralizing in tendency, and because they are perverted by designing and corrupt men to wrongful and mischievous purposes, and liable to become potent and dangerous engines of evil.

RESOLVED, That correct principles and praiseworthy objects do not require a veil of secrecy, and can be sustained and accomplished without their advocates being banded together by illegal oaths and obligations.

RESOLVED, That as American citizens, devotedly attached to the Free Institutions of our country, we value as above all price, the rights of conscience and judgment—the liberty to act as our judgment shall dictate, and as long as we are FREE will never surrender to any midnight or mid-day conclave, the power to determine to whom we shall give, or from whom we shall withhold our votes.

Resolved, That the oaths, obligations, and objects, (as developed in the Legislative Senatorial debate,) of the political and secret organization in this State, under the control of James W. Barker, popularly known as Hindoo-Know-Nothings, are startling in their character and should arouse and alarm every reflecting mind.

Resolved, That we deeply regret that at this peculiar crisis, when the great interests of Human Freedom are at stake, Slavery finds a powerful ally in this Hindoo organization.

Resolved, That, as it is evident that the pro-slavery Democrats and the ultra silver grey Whigs of our State have secretly abandoned their respective parties, and formed a sworn alliance around the altars of Hindooism, the sole object of which is to put the brethren of the second and third degree, in political place and power, a union of action of ALL opposed to such secret political organizations, should be had for self-protection.

Resolved, That to effectually rebuke the outrage perpetrated by the repeal of the Missouri Compromise, and to restore to Freedom its violated rights, we earnestly recommend the combined and united political action of all the friends of Truth, Freedom and Justice.

Resolved, That entertaining these views, and having an abiding conviction that they are truthful and right, disregarding all considerations of temporary policy, WE OPENLY PROCLAIM THEM, well aware of the fact that there is a secret political organization in our town, claiming to have the power to control its political destinies.

Resolved, That James Stewart, William Boyd, Nicholas Robertson, Benjamin Skellie, and Edward Dodd, be appointed to call a meeting of all the electors of the town of Argyle, who approve of the principles of the foregoing resolutions, to be held at the house of J. Rouse, on Monday, the 26th inst., at 2 o'clock, P. M., to nominate candidates for town officers.   WM. D. ROBERTSON, Chairman.
EBENEZER CAMPBELL, Secy.

Town Meeting.

The Electors of the town of Argyle, irrespective of former party distinctions, who approve of the principles of the above resolutions, are requested to meet at the house of J. ROUSE, in the Village of Argyle, on Monday, the 26th inst., at 2 P. M., to nominate Candidates for town Offices.
March 21, 1855.
JAMES STEWART,
WILLIAM BOYD,
NICHOLAS ROBERTSON,
BENJAMIN SKELLIE,
EDWARD DODD,
Committee

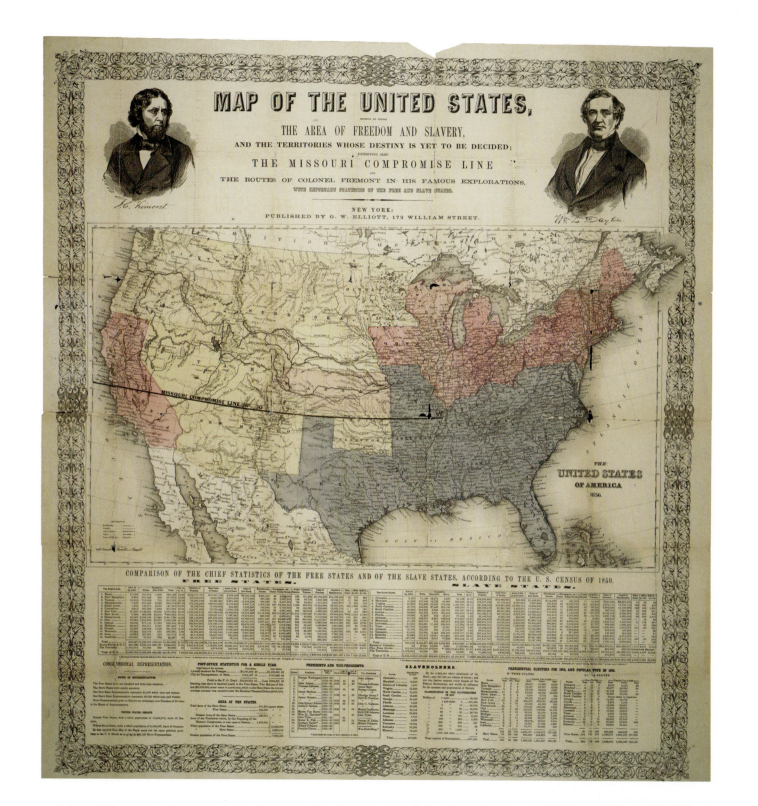

41

DRED SCOTT, ARTIST UNKNOWN, OIL
ON CANVAS, AFTER 1857
Dred Scott (c.1795–1858) was a
slave who protested his continuing
servitude on the grounds that he
had lived for several years in the free
territory of Wisconsin—where slavery
had been prohibited by the Missouri
Compromise. The case came before
the Supreme Court, which ruled in
1857 that the ban on slavery in the
territories was unconstitutional. It
also stated that slaves were property
and that the Constitution protected
the right of property. The Dred Scott
decision energized antislavery factions
in the North and helped to solidify
the Republican Party. The New
York State legislature vehemently
denounced the decision and proposed
"An Act To Secure Freedom To All
Persons Within This State," which
passed in the assembly but lost in the
Senate for want of action at the close
of the session.
(New-York Historical Society)

42

New York Divided

New Yorkers were divided by more than slavery during the 1850s. Upstate evangelical Protestants opposed immigration, particularly Irish and German Catholics. Many evangelicals joined nativist groups and temperance organizations and gravitated to the emerging Republican Party. Immigrants themselves tended to locate in downstate cities, particularly New York, where they attached themselves to Democratic political machines, such as Tammany Hall. Immigrants were fearful that emancipation might threaten their jobs, and neighborhoods tended to be hostile to blacks.

Various ballots from 1850s gubernatorial campaigns
In the 1850s there were more than sixteen different parties running in New York's various gubernatorial elections. These paper ballots (also known as party tickets) were issued by specific parties and handed out to voters to drop in the election box. Ballots such as these made it difficult for people to "split the ticket." Paper ballots were not standardized until 1888 with the election of Grover Cleveland. *(New York State Museum Collection)*

1852

STATE.
For Governor,
WASHINGTON HUNT.
For Lieutenant Governor,
WILLIAM KENT.
For Canal Commissioner,
THOMAS KEMPSHALL.
For Inspector of State Prisons,
EPENETUS CROSBY.
For Representative in Congress,
ORSAMUS B. MATTESON.
For Sheriff,
JOHN B. BRADT.
For County Clerk,
ALEXANDER RAE.
For Superintendent of the Poor,
WILLIAM LEWIS.
For Sessions,
CHARLES ROBINSON.
For Coroners,
SAMUEL H. ADDINGTON
JOHN O'NEILL,
WARREN D. ROWLE...

STATE
For Governor,
Horatio Seymour.
For Lieutenant Governor,
Henry J. Raymond.
For Canal Commissioner,
Henry Fitzhugh.
For State Prison Inspector,
Norwood Bowne.
For Representative in Congress,
Thomas T. Flagler.
For Member of Assembly,
Alexis Ward.
For County Clerk,
Arad Thomas,
For County Treasurer,
Ambrose Wood.
For County Superintendent of the Poor,
John F. Sawyer.
For Justice of Sessions,
John H. White.

STATE.
For Governor,
MINTHORNE TOMPKINS.
For Lieutenant Governor,
SETH M. GATES.
For Canal Commissioner,
CHARLES A. WHEATON.
For State Prison Inspector,
GEORGE CURTISS.
For Representative in Congress,
JAMES C. DELONG.
For Sheriff,
ELLIS ELLIS.
For County Clerk,
HENRY N. PORTER.
For Superintendent of the Poor,
ELIAS D. PORTER.
For Justices of Sessions,
DANIEL W. CLARK,
WILLIAM WALKER.
For Coroners,
WILLIAM P. ST. JOHN,
ARBA BLAIR,
JAMES M. SIMMONS.

1854

State.
American...
For Governor,
Daniel Ullma...
For Lieutenant G...
Gustavus A...
For Canal Com...
Clark Burn...
For Inspector of ...
James P. S...
For Representa...
William H...
For County ...
John Wh...
For Superintend...

STATE.
For Governor,
Horatio Seymour.
For Lieutenant Governor,
William H. Ludlow,
For Canal Commissioner,
Jason Clark
For Inspector of State Prisons,
William R. Andrews,
For Representative in Congress,
George Hastings
For County Treasurer,
Walter E. Landerdale...

For Governor,
Myron H. Clark.
For Lieutenant Governor,
Henry J. Raymond.
For Canal Commissioner,
Henry Fitzhugh.
For Inspector of State Prisons,
Norwood Bowne.
Representative in Congress,
William H. Kelsey.
For County Treasure...

1856

STATE.
For Governor,
MYRON H. CLARK.
For Lieutenant Governor,
HENRY J RAYMOND.
For Canal Commissioner,
HENRY FITZHUGH.
For Inspector of State Prisons,
NORWOOD BOWNE.
For Representative in Congress,
ORSAMUS B. MATTESON.
For County Clerk,
LUMAN KIMBALL,
For Justice for Sessions,
NORRIS WILCOX.
For Superintendent of the Poor,
VINCENT TAFT.
For Coroner,
EDWARD H. FRANCIS.

Democratic Ticket.
STATE.
For Governor,
Amasa J. Pa...
For Lieutenant Gover...
John Vander...
For Canal Commissi...
John L. Ru...
For State Prison In...
Matthew T...
For Clerk of the Co...
Horatio G...
For Representative...
Benjamin...
For District Attor...
John A...
For County Treas...
Walter F...
For Coroner,
Arnold...
For Justice of S...
Clark F...

STATE.
For Governor,
John A. King.
For Lieutenant Governor,
Henry R. Selden.
For Canal Commissioner,
Charles H. Sherrill.
For Inspector of State Prisons,
Wesley Bailey.
For Clerk of the Court of Appeals,
Russell F. Hicks.
For Representative in Congress,
William C. Johnson.
For District Attorney,
James H. Munger...

STATE.
For Governor,
Erastus Brooks.
For Lieutenant Governor,
Lyman Odell.
For Canal Commissioner,
...rescott
...te Prisons
...anders
...of Appeals.
...Mann
...Congress,
...allett
...torney,
...rd
...reasurer,
...mmatt
...dge
...omas.

Temperance

As a result of the reforms spreading across the state, many New Yorkers supported temperance, the abstinence from alcohol. In 1829, the New York State Temperance Society was founded with seventy-eight branches across the state.

Temperance was also supported by nativists, who viewed Irish and German immigrants as drunkards. It was an important issue that competed with and surpassed antislavery for the voters' attention. New York temperance forces were led by Whig leader Myron H. Clark of Canandaigua. The 1854 legislature passed a prohibition bill by a large margin, only to have it vetoed by Governor Seymour on constitutional grounds.

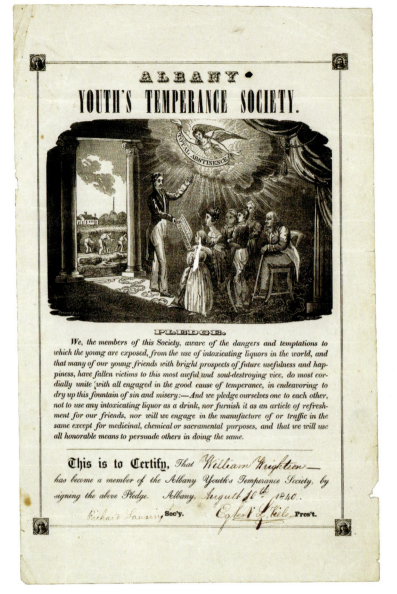

CERTIFICATE OF MEMBERSHIP, ALBANY YOUTH TEMPERANCE SOCIETY, 1840, *above*
(New York State Library, Manuscripts and Special Collections)

TEMPERANCE CARD, 1858, *left*
(New York State Museum Collection, H-1978.126.9)

TEMPERANCE AND REFORM.

TO THE VOTERS OF THE SIXTEENTH WARD.

THE day is fast approaching when the Electors of this State will be called to the polls for the purpose of giving their verdict on questions of public polity by electing officers of the State and City Governments, basing their choice of candidates on the principles which they severally represent.

The Executive Committee of **THE SIXTEENTH WARD TEMPERANCE ALLIANCE**, in view of this fact, and of the monstrous evils under which our City and State labor from the policy adopted by both the great parties of the country, and after careful deliberation, have selected candidates for the several local offices from among those of their fellow-citizens who are not participants in, or supporters of, the wrongs complained of, and for whom they ask your undivided friendship and support. The names of these candidates, and the offices for which they are respectively nominated, may be found below.

ANDREW LESTER, the candidate for Representative in Congress, is well known as one of our most active and respected merchants—a man who is *practically* acquainted with the wants of a mercantile community, and fully competent to represent the Emporium of the Union, in the National Council, *as it should be represented.* As a practical man, his claims to your support are based on no *fictitious theory*, nor does he see our necessities through a lawyer's or a schoolmaster's spectacles. Without pretension and without ambition, he has not sought the position which, through the confidence of his neighbors, he has been called to occupy; yet his modest merit will add dignity to the honors which we ask for him at your hands, and redound no less to the honor of those who give, than to him who would receive them.

GEORGE T. LEACH, the candidate for the Assembly, is no stranger. A hard-working mechanic, respected by all who know him, *for his own sake*, and for the sake of his generous labors for the public good, he is presented for your support with confidence and pride. Should you see fit to endorse our choice, we assure you that an honest, unbought delegate will be secured to the District.

HENRY B. DAWSON, who heads the Charter Ticket, as our candidate for the office of Assistant Alderman, is also well known as an active friend of Temperance and Radical Reform. On the other side of this sheet he speaks for himself as to his proposed line of action, and no comments from us are needed to illustrate the subject. That he will strive to do his duty, need not be told to those who know him.

WHITMAN PHILLIPS, the candidate for Assessor, and HUGH S. DUNN and CORNELIUS R. CHICHESTER, our candidates for Constables, have been long and favorably known to the citizens of the Ward, and will, therefore, need no further commendation from us.

For these men we ask your votes and your sympathy. We ask it in behalf of the best interests of our City and State; we ask in behalf of political honesty—in behalf of humanity. We leave the matter with you, hoping you will not falter in doing your duty as your *judgment* dictates.

For Congress,	ANDREW LESTER.
For Assembly,	GEORGE T. LEACH.
For Assistant Alderman,	HENRY B. DAWSON.
For Assessor,	WHITMAN PHILLIPS.
For Constables,	HUGH S. DUNN,
	CORNELIUS R. CHICHESTER.

N. B. Preserve the enclosed Tickets, and deposit them in the Ballot-Boxes on Tuesday, Nov. 2d.

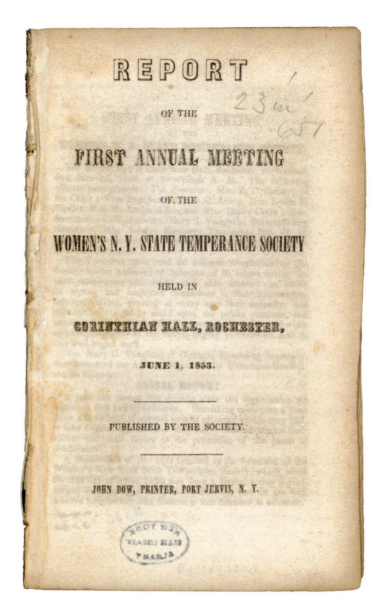

REPORT

OF THE

FIRST ANNUAL MEETING

OF THE

WOMEN'S N. Y. STATE TEMPERANCE SOCIETY

HELD IN

CORINTHIAN HALL, ROCHESTER,

JUNE 1, 1853.

PUBLISHED BY THE SOCIETY.

JOHN DOW, PRINTER, PORT JERVIS, N. Y.

TEMPERANCE AND REFORM—TO THE VOTERS OF THE 16TH WARD (NEW YORK CITY), BROADSIDE, 1852
(New York State Library, Manuscripts and Special Collections)

WOMEN'S NYS TEMPERANCE SOCIETY, FIRST ANNUAL REPORT ROCHESTER, 1853
(New York State Library, Manuscripts and Special Collections)

COTTON FLAG, 1844
This flag was carried in the Native American Procession of 1844. The Native American Democratic Association developed into the American Republican Party. In 1844, James Harper, the party's candidate, won the mayoral election in New York City. *(New-York Historical Society)*

Nativism

Since the early nineteenth century, native-born citizens viewed immigrants—who subscribed to different religious beliefs, spoke different languages, and competed with native New Yorkers for jobs—with apprehension. Nativism grew stronger in the 1840s and early 1850s, when more than three million foreigners entered the United States, many through New York Harbor. In 1854, anti-immigrant sentiment coalesced around the Know-Nothing Party. Later called the American Party, it campaigned on an anti-Catholic and temperance agenda, often with the support of upstate evangelicals.

Founding of the Republican Party in New York

Divisions over the issue of slavery during the 1850s led to the dissolution of the Whig Party as a serious force in national politics. To fill this void, opponents of the proposed Kansas-Nebraska Act gathered in January 1854 in New York City. The meeting resulted in a statewide convention in August in Saratoga Springs. Drawing support from former Whigs, antislavery Democrats, and members of the Free Soil Party, the newly-named Republicans adopted an antislavery platform, though they fell short of creating a new political party.

The following year, the Republicans gained the backing of Horace Greeley and his *New York Tribune*. With this support, the Republicans captured the New York Governor's office in 1856—holding their first national convention that same year. By 1860, the Republicans controlled most of New York's statewide offices. At the 1860 Presidential Convention, the New York State Delegation advocated the nomination of U.S. Senator William Seward.

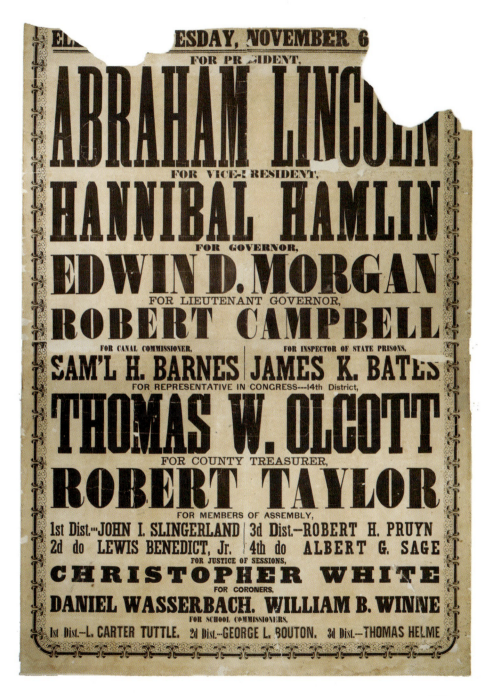

REPUBLICAN CANDIDATES IN ALBANY COUNTY, 1860
Mobilizing around the theme "free soil, free men," the Republican Party opposed the expansion of slavery to the Western Territories. New York Republicans met for the first time in Syracuse in 1855, appointing an equal number of former Whigs and Democrats for the 1856 campaign ticket.
(New York State Library, Manuscripts and Special Collections)

William H. Seward, 1801–1872
Governor, Senator, Secretary of State

William Henry Seward served as governor of New York (1839–1842), United States senator (1849–1861), and secretary of state (1861–1869). He was born in Florida, Orange County.

As senator, Seward established himself as a leader in the national debate over slavery. He was a driving force in the establishment of the Republican Party and a leading contender for

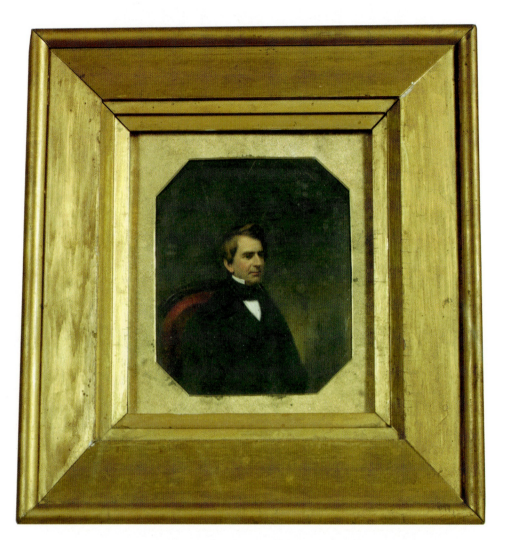

WILLIAM H. SEWARD, ARTIST UNKNOWN, OIL ON BOARD, C. 1850
This painting depicts Seward shortly after he was governor of New York State. *(New York State Museum Collection, H-1973.4.1)*

WILLIAM H. SEWARD, BY CHAUNCEY BRADLEY IVES, MARBLE, C. 1880
After serving as Secretary of State (1861–1869), Seward retired to Auburn, New York, where he lived until his death in 1872. Today his house is open to the public. *(New York State Museum Collection, H-XX.357.5)*

its presidential nomination in 1860. Despite his loss to Abraham Lincoln, likely due to his antislavery activism, Seward became a loyal member of Lincoln's wartime cabinet. He prevented foreign intervention early in the war and advised Lincoln on the crafting of the Emancipation Proclamation.

CAMPAIGN COIN, PIN BACK, AND BALLOT FOR
WILLIAM H. SEWARD
William Seward (Whig Party) served two terms as governor from 1839 to 1842. *(New York State Museum Collection, H-2006.71.9–10, 12)*

STATE.

For Governor
William H. Seward.
For Lieutenant Governor
Luther Bradish.
For Senator
Bethuel Peck.

CONGRESS.

For Congress
Anson Brown.

COUNTY.

For Assembly
Calvin Wheeler
John Stewart.

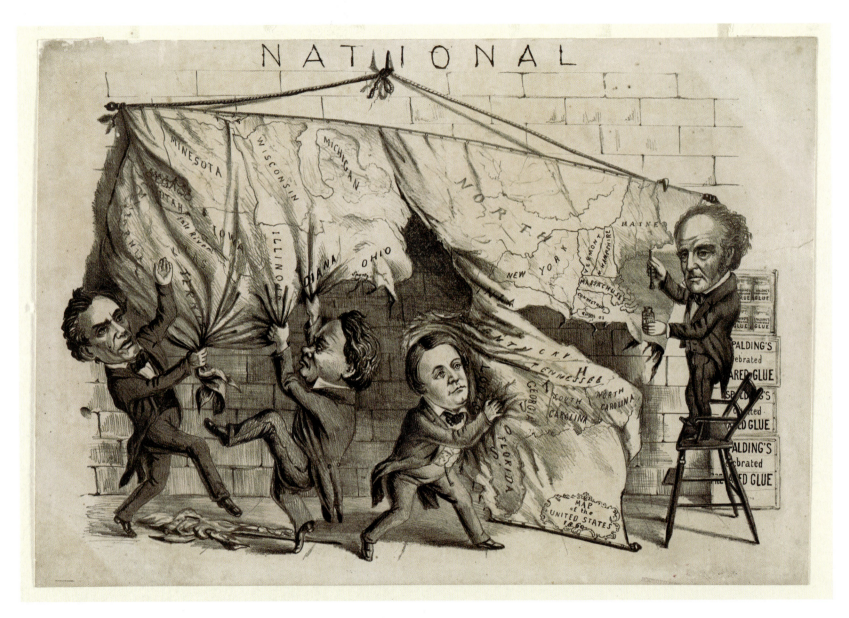

"DIVIDING THE NATIONAL MAP," 1860

This cartoon shows three of the four presidential candidates in 1860—(left to right) Republican Abraham Lincoln, Democrat Stephen A. Douglas, and Southern Democrat John C. Breckinridge—tearing the country apart, while the fourth, Constitutional Union candidate John Bell, applies glue from a tiny, useless pot. Lincoln won more than half the electoral votes but only 40 percent of the popular vote. (Library of Congress)

Election of 1860

New York played an important role in the presidential election of 1860, one of the most important in American history. Stephen A. Douglas made a respectable showing, but Abraham Lincoln, the Republican candidate, won New York's thirty-five electoral votes. Other New York Republicans, including sitting governor Edwin Morgan and a majority in both houses of the legislature, also fared well. Lincoln's election to the presidency set the nation on an inevitable course toward civil war.

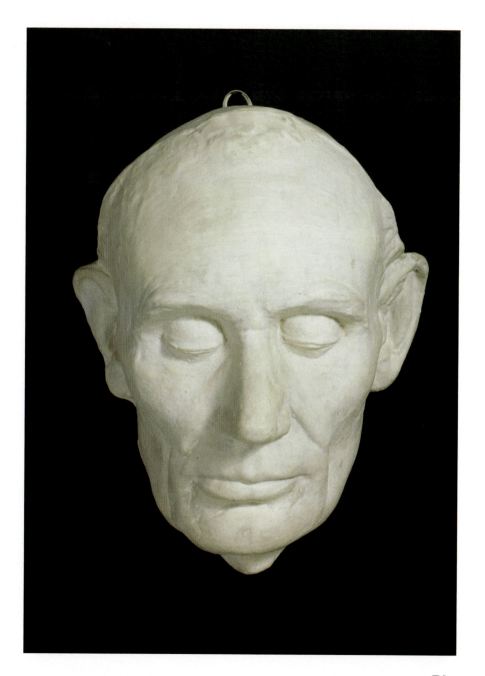

ABRAHAM LINCOLN, LIFE MASK, PAINTED PLASTER, 1860
This cast was part of the Phrenological Museum of Fowler & Wells, which opened in New York City in 1842. Brothers Orson Squire Fowler and Lorenzo Niles Fowler and their business associate Samuel Roberts Wells were noted phrenologists who read heads to understand the subjects' "temperaments."
(New-York Historical Society)

ABRAHAM LINCOLN, UNKNOWN ARTIST,
OIL ON CANVAS, C.1860
New York was divided over the 1860
election. Abraham Lincoln received only
53 percent of the vote in the state while
Stephen A. Douglas received 46 percent.
*(New York State Museum Collection,
H-1943.7.1)*

The Civil War, 1861–1865

Aaron Noble

The Empire State at War

When examining the traditional measures used to gauge New Yorkers' support for the war effort—"blood and treasure"—the state provided more to the Union than any other. New York provided more soldiers to the Union armies and more New Yorkers gave their lives in the conflict than any state; its citizens paid more taxes to fund the war effort, and gave more money to charity and relief organizations. New Yorkers also purchased the most war bonds of any state. New York industries played a critical role in arming, feeding, and clothing the United States Army. New York agricultural output was a "breadbasket of the Union." New York's extensive railroads and canal system transported men and materiel to the front lines of the war. This same transportation network transported more than ten thousand Confederate prisoners of war to the prison camp at Elmira.

New York was the largest state in the Union. With a population of 3.8 million people, which was approximately 17 percent of the total U.S. population in 1860, the state boasted the largest militia in the country. When Fort Sumter was fired upon in April 1861, the New York State Militia totaled 19,189 officers and men. The United States Army had only 16,006 men at this time, and only about five hundred of those were stationed along the eastern seaboard.

While united in battle to preserve the nation, New Yorkers were torn over the same issues that had divided them before the war. In order for the North to emerge

THE DEPARTURE OF THE 7TH REGIMENT, TO THE WAR, APRIL 19, 1861, 1869.
THOMAS NAST (1840–1902)
(New York State Military Museum, Division of Military and Naval Affairs)

victorious, however, these divisions—between immigrant and native-born, rich and poor, abolitionist and anti-abolitionist, Republican and Democrat—had to be overcome.

By the end of the war in 1865, New York had committed 448,000 troops to the Union cause—approximately 16 percent of the total number of Union soldiers. More than 53,000 New Yorkers died from wounds and from disease; more than any state on either side of the conflict.

"Rally 'Round the Flag" (1861) Secession Winter

The election of Abraham Lincoln prompted several Southern states to secede from the Union. While Lincoln had not advocated for abolition in his campaign, and had stated that he would support slavery's continuation if dissolution of the Union was the alternative, many believed the Republican victory signaled the end of Southern political power and with it, the ultimate end of slavery in the United States. On December 20, 1860, South Carolina became the first state to leave the Union. By February, seven states in the Deep South had seceded and formed a separate government, the Confederate States of America.

Tensions mounted as the inauguration approached. Confederate troops seized U.S. forts across the South. In Charleston, South Carolina, the U.S. commander, Major Robert Anderson, withdrew all his troops into Fort Sumter, located on an island in the harbor. Cut off from supplies, Anderson informed the newly sworn-in president of the low provisions. Both sides viewed Fort Sumter as a line in the sand.

FERNANDO WOOD
Mayor, New York

MAYOR FERNANDO WOODS
On January 6, 1861, Mayor Fernando Wood recommended that New York City and Long Island secede from the rest of New York and establish themselves as a free port open to trade with Southern plantation owners. The proposal was rejected.
(New York State Library, Manuscripts and Special Collections)

"FORT SUMTER, SEEN FROM THE REAR AT LOW WATER"
An engraved drawing of Fort Sumter, *Harper's Weekly*, January 26, 1861
(New York State Library, Manuscripts and Special Collections)

Lincoln in New York—the Inaugural Train

On February 11, a train bearing President-elect Lincoln left Illinois for the nation's capital. During the journey, Lincoln's train stopped in Westfield, Buffalo, and Syracuse. At Albany, Lincoln addressed the State Legislature before proceeding to New York City.

"I still have confidence that the Almighty, the Maker of the Universe will, through the instrumentality of this great and intelligent people, bring us through this as He has through all other difficulties of our country."

—*Abraham Lincoln, February 18, 1861, address to the New York State Legislature at Albany*

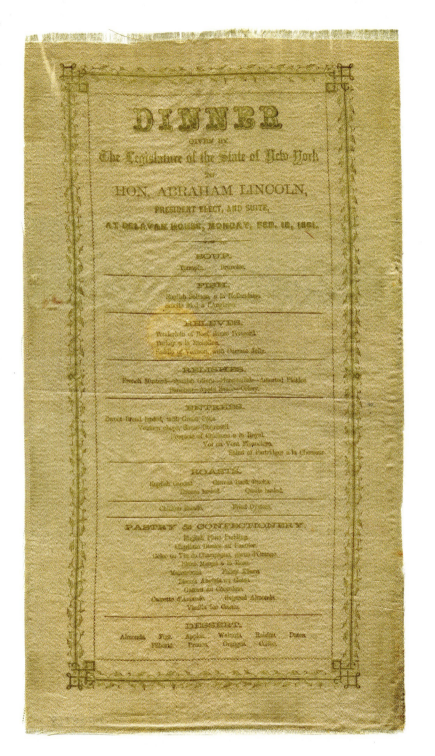

MENU
This silk menu commemorates a dinner given by the Legislature of the State of New York to honor Abraham Lincoln, president-elect, at Delavan House, Monday, February 18, 1861.
(New York State Library, Manuscripts and Special Collections)

LINCOLN IN BUFFALO
At each stop along his route, the president-elect was greeted by large, cheering crowds. In New York City, Lincoln remarked to Mayor Wood his gratitude for the reception even in a city "who do not by a majority agree with me in political sentiments."
(Library of Congress)

GOVERNOR MORGAN
(New York State Library, Manuscripts and Special Collections)

Governor Edwin Morgan

Born in Berkshire County, Massachusetts, Edwin Morgan moved to New York, where he became a successful merchant and banker. He was elected to the New York State Senate in 1850. He was an early proponent of the Republican Party and became its first chairman in 1856. During the election of 1860, Morgan was instrumental in drumming up support for the Republican candidate, Abraham Lincoln.

GOVERNOR MORGAN REVIEWING 1ST DIVISION
This *New-York Illustrated News* drawing depicts Governor Morgan in Manhattan reviewing the troops in early March 1861. *(New York State Library, Manuscripts and Special Collections)*

During the secession crisis, Governor Morgan readied the State Militia in case of war. He needed to raise, arm, and equip vast numbers of troops, prepare the state's industries to supply the war effort, and work on financing the conflict.

Morgan drafted a bill that raised two million dollars in state income tax to provision thirty thousand volunteer soldiers. A newly created Military Board was charged with raising and equipping these troops. Morgan was commissioned a major general of U.S. Volunteers by President Lincoln, solidifying his reputation as the state's "War Governor."

Fort Sumter

Following the secession of South Carolina on December 20, the commander of the U.S. Army troops stationed in Charleston, Major Robert Anderson, ordered his men to withdraw into Fort Sumter at the center of the harbor on December 26, 1860. The fort was surrounded by soldiers of the South Carolina militia, later to be joined by the newly established Confederate States Army.

On March 4, Abraham Lincoln was sworn in as the nation's sixteenth president. He was almost immediately informed of the dire state of provisions at Fort Sumter. Lincoln informed the

SHIPMENT OF MILITARY STORES ON BOARD THE STEAMSHIP *Baltic* AT NEW YORK, APRIL 6, 1861
President Lincoln ordered ships from New York to resupply Fort Sumter. In an attempt not to incite Confederate reaction, he did not send reinforcements. *Harper's Weekly*, April 20, 1861
(*New York State Library, Manuscripts and Special Collections*)

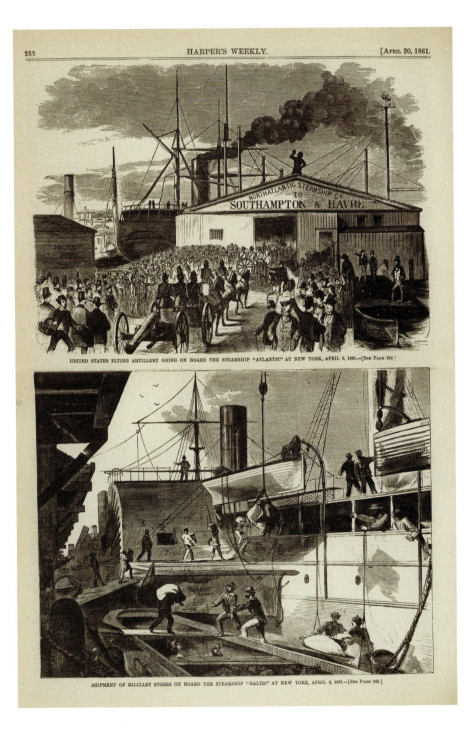

UNITED STATES FLYING ARTILLERY GOING ON BOARD THE STEAMSHIP "ATLANTIC" AT NEW YORK, APRIL 6, 1861.—[SEE PAGE 246.]

SHIPMENT OF MILITARY STORES ON BOARD THE STEAMSHIP "BALTIC" AT NEW YORK, APRIL 8, 1861.—[SEE PAGE 246.]

THE BOMBARDMENT OF FORT SUMTER,
News of the bombardment of Fort Sumter by Rebel artillery shocked the nation. *Harper's Weekly*, April 20, 1861
(New York State Library, Manuscripts and Special Collections)

"The curtain has fallen upon the first act. . . . Fort Sumpter [*sic*] has been surrendered and the Stars and Stripes of the American Republic give place to the felon flag of the Southern Confederates."
—*New York Times*, April 15, 1861

MEDALLION
New York City's Chamber of Commerce ordered this medallion to be struck and presented to the defenders of Fort Sumter as they arrived in New York City. The medallion features Major Robert Anderson atop the ramparts at the captured fort.
(New York State Museum Collection, H-1975.47.1)

government of South Carolina of his intention to resupply the fort. In an effort to prevent hostilities, he promised not to send reinforcements. On April 12, 1861, Confederate troops opened fire on Fort Sumter. By April 14, the fort's garrison was forced to surrender. Sumter's defenders sailed from Charleston to New York City where they received a hero's welcome.

TO ARMS! TO ARMS!!

OUR COUNTRY CALLS, WE SHOULD OBEY!

The Citizens of the Village of

AND VICINITY WILL HOLD AN

UNION MEETING,

At   On

It is earnestly requested, and expected that all Patriotic, and law loving Citizens will be present. The object of the meeting is to recruit brave men to suppress this most fratricidal rebellion. The meeting will be addressed by prominent Citizens, also

M. E. CORNELL,

Late Lieut. of the Cleaveland Light Artillery, who is Commissioned to raise a

COMPANY OF CAVALRY

for the *"Ira Harris Guards."* Arouse ye---valiant men of Western New York, and avenge the old flag of '76 which has been trampled upon by an infatuated mob of ruthless traitors. Flock thou *Sons of Freedom* to the rescue of the American Eagle, that choosen bird of Liberty, which now screams through the land, for your aid.

M. E. CORNELL,   S. S. CORNELL,   J. H. C. LYNCH.

S. F. JORY, PRINTER, OVER DR. SALMONS' STORE, LIMA, N. Y.

The Call to Arms

On April 15, 1861, President Lincoln issued a call for 75,000 volunteers to quell the Southern rebellion, prompting four more states to leave the Union. The outbreak of the war and Virginia's secession made Washington, D.C., vulnerable to attack. Governor Morgan faced the daunting task of mobilizing the state's population for war in order to raise and equip large numbers of troops to send to Washington.

Lincoln requested that New York gather seventeen regiments—13,280 men—to help defend the Union and suppress the rebellion. Many believed the war would be decided with a single, dramatic battle. The state legislature authorized raising thirty thousand troops.

As New Yorkers from all political parties and economic classes rallied to the federal cause, they looked to the national flag as a symbol of unity. Any debate over leniency toward the South disappeared in a wave of patriotic fervor. With flags waving, New Yorkers marched to war at Union Square in Manhattan and in every corner of the state.

BROADSIDE—"TO ARMS!"—LIMA
Recruitment broadside from Lima, Livingston County.
(New York State Museum Collection, H-1976.191.2)

Our Banner in the Sky (1861), BY FREDERICK CHURCH
Renowned New York artist Frederick Church painted this work in response to the patriotism that swept across the North in the wake of the attack on Fort Sumter.
(New York State Office of Parks, Recreation and Historic Preservation)

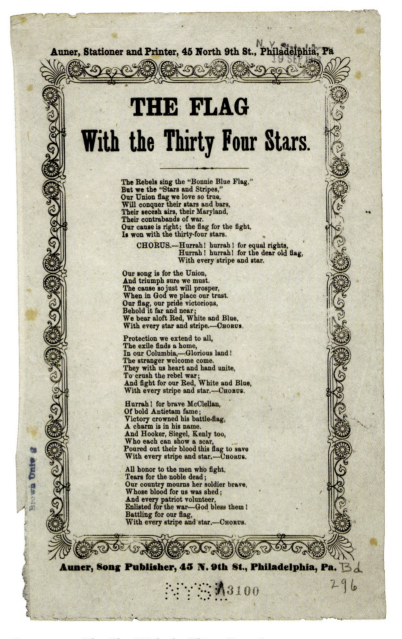

BROADSIDE, ARE YOU READY TO STAND BY THE STARS AND STRIPES?
This April 18, 1861, broadside from Glens Falls, New York, called for patriotic citizens to defend the Union.
(New York State Library, Manuscripts and Special Collections)

SONGSHEET, *The Flag With the Thirty Four Stars*
In 1861, the United States included thirty-four states. Despite the secession of eleven Southern states, the national banner remained unchanged until the addition of West Virginia in 1863.
(New York State Library, Manuscripts and Special Collections)

HEIGHT MEASURING DEVICE
This device was used to measure a recruit's height when he enlisted in the Army. The tallest Union soldier was 6'11" and the shortest was 3'4". The average height of a Union soldier was 5'8".
(Onondaga Historical Association)

THE GREAT RALLY AT UNION SQUARE
Thousands rally at Union Square in New York City in an outpouring of support for the Union cause.
(New York State Library, Manuscripts and Special Collections)

"NATIONAL GUARD" CARTRIDGE BOX
This cartridge box was carried by a soldier in the 7th Regiment, New York State Militia. The "NG" monogram on the cartridge box refers to the regiment's nickname, the National Guard. It was adopted in 1824 in honor of the American Revolutionary War hero the Marquis de Lafayette, who commanded "Le Garde Nationale" during the French Revolution. In 1903, Congress enacted a militia law renaming all state militias the National Guard. *(New York State Museum Collection, H-1947.4.11)*

Foreigners, Fenians, and "Forty-Eighters"
New York's Ethnic Volunteers

Thousands of immigrants answered President Lincoln's call for volunteers because they believed they would gain favor by serving in combat. In all, New York fielded twenty-three "ethnic" regiments, and thousands more served in other units. Nearly 30 percent of New York soldiers were foreign-born.

Many of the immigrants who fought in the war had left Europe for political reasons. Many former military officers fled the German states following the failed democratic revolutions of 1848. Many Fenians (Irish Nationalists) came to the United States hoping to raise men and money to liberate their country from British rule.

> "We [Germans] know too well, from experience in their dear fatherland, what it is to have a country torn asunder and divided into many small kingdoms and principalities."
>
> —*Rudolph Augustus Witthaus, German-American Leader in New York, exhorting fellow immigrants to defend the Union*

SONGSHEET, *Our German Volunteers*
41,179 German immigrants served in New York's volunteer regiments during the war. *(New York State Museum Collection, H-1974.27.4)*

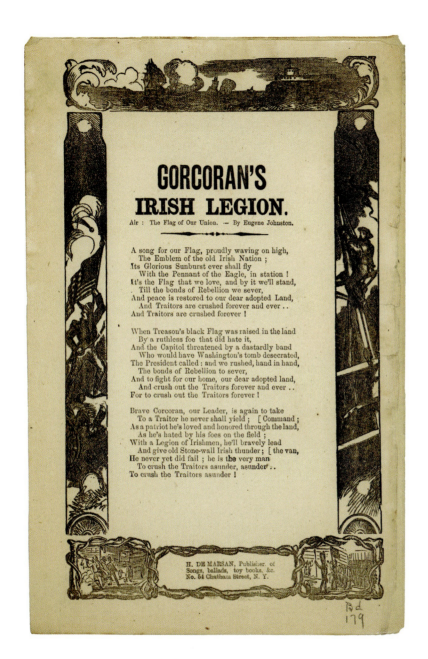

HAT BADGE, 69TH NEW YORK, *above left* The 69th New York Volunteers became part of the Irish Brigade and fought in nearly all of the major battles with the Army of the Potomac, suffering nearly five hundred casualties. *(New York State Museum Collection)*

HAT BADGE, 39TH NEW YORK, *above right* This hat badge was created for the 39th New York Volunteer Infantry, nicknamed "The Garibaldi Guard." *(New York State Museum Collection)*

SONGSHEET, *Corcoran's Irish Legion*
Among New York's volunteer soldiers were 42,095 Irish immigrants.
(New York State Library, Manuscripts and Special Collections)

MUSTER ROLL ABSTRACT, EMANUEL GOMEZ
Muster roll abstract for Emanuel Gomez, possibly a Latino or Sephardic Jewish soldier serving with the 39th Regiment, New York Volunteers.
(New York State Archives)

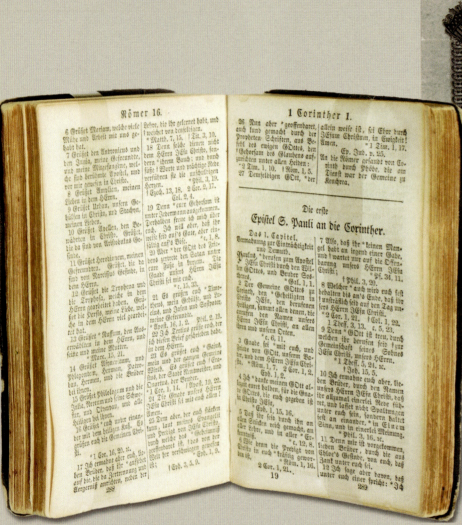

BIBLE

This German language Bible was distributed to New York soldiers by the New York Bible Society. It was carried by William Wooltje of Company F, 186th New York Volunteer Infantry from Lewis County.
(New York State Museum Collection, H-1971.36.2)

COMMISSION

Commission signed by Governor Morgan to Philippe Régis Denis de Keredern de Trobriand, a French aristocrat who immigrated to New York City. During the war, de Trobriand commanded the 55th New York Volunteer Infantry, a regiment largely composed of French expatriates known as the Gardes Lafayette.
(New York State Military Museum, Division of Military and Naval Affairs)

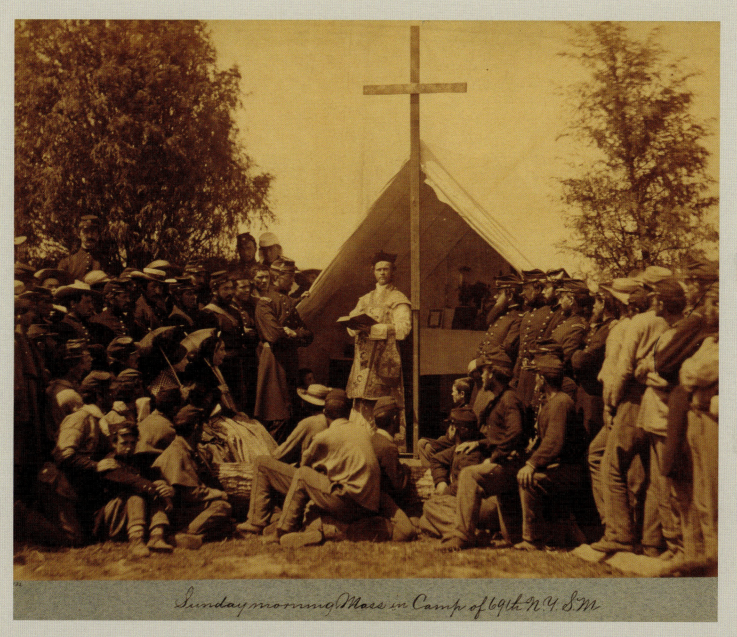

Sunday morning Mass in Camp of 69th N.Y.S.M.

SUNDAY MORNING MASS IN CAMP OF 69TH
Members of the predominantly Irish Catholic 69th New York observe Mass near the nation's capital in 1861. Five thousand men volunteered to join the 69th New York in April 1861. *(Library of Congress)*

RECONNOISSANCE BY COLONEL MAX WEBER'S TURNER RIFLES IN THE VICINITY OF NEWMARKET BRIDGE, ON THE ROAD TO YORKTOWN, VA.

RECONNAISSANCE OF COLONEL MAX WEBER'S GERMAN TURNER RIFLE REGIMENT, 20TH NEW YORK VOLUNTEERS
While most German immigrants in New York voted Democratic during the election of 1860, they resoundingly opposed secession. The 20th New York Volunteer Infantry served at the battles of Antietam and Fredericksburg before being discharged in New York City. *New York State Library, Manuscripts and Special Collections)*

THE GARIBALDI ZOUAVES ON THE DOUBLE-QUICK IN BROADWAY.—[See Page 359.]

The Garibaldi Zouaves on the Double-Quick in Broadway

New York City's immigrants raised a multiethnic regiment that included 1,086 men from at least eleven different nationalities. The men of the 39th New York Volunteers honored their Italian heritage by naming the unit for Giuseppe Garibaldi, a military leader who led the quest for Italian unification. Garibaldi was residing in exile in Brooklyn. *Harper's Weekly*, June 8, 1861 *(New York State Library, Manuscripts and Special Collections)*

79th New York, "The Cameron Highlanders"

Most men of the 79th Regiment, New York State Militia, were Scottish immigrants. Many were British Army veterans of the Crimean War (1853–1856). The Highlanders immediately enlisted into Federal service after the attack on Fort Sumter. They first saw action at Bull Run, where they bore the brunt of a Confederate counterattack. In total, 199 men were killed, wounded, or missing.

UNIFORM COAT, SPORRAN, AND GLENGARRY
At the start of the war, militia uniforms often varied widely. The 79th New York adopted the Glengarry hat and traditional Scottish sporrans. The unit trimmed their uniforms in Cameronian tartan patterns in honor of their heritage and their commanding officer.
(New-York Historical Society)

THE 79TH REGIMENT, NEW YORK STATE MILITIA, MARCHING THROUGH THE STREETS OF NEW YORK CITY
The 79th Regiment, New York State Militia, clad in a distinctive dress uniform that included Glengarries, kilts, and sporrans. Before going to war, the kilts were replaced with tartan trousers. *Harper's Weekly*, May 25, 1861
(New York State Library, Manuscripts and Special Collections)

New York's Native Peoples in the Civil War

During the 1830s and 1840s, the U.S. Government forced the relocation of Native Americans in the East. Thousands were evicted from their ancestral homelands and moved westward onto reservations. Despite this treatment, twenty thousand Native Americans volunteered to serve on both sides of the Civil War. In New York, six hundred Iroquois—from all six nations—served in the Union Army. Many of these soldiers fought to preserve the Union, in hope of also preserving their remaining homelands.

FLANK MARKER
Flank marker of the 132nd New York Volunteer Infantry Regiment, part of which was recruited from the Allegany, Cattaraugus, and Tuscarora Reservations. *(New York State Military Museum, Division of Military and Naval Affairs)*

MUSTER ROLL ABSTRACT, WILLIAM KENNEDY

Private William Kennedy, a Native American from Western New York, enlisted in Company D, 132nd New York Volunteer Infantry at Buffalo in July 1862. He was captured at Bachelors Creek, North Carolina, on February 1, 1864, and died at Andersonville Prison, Georgia, on September 27, 1864. *(New York State Archives)*

The First Martyr

On May 23, 1861, Virginia voted to secede from the United States. Union troops, including the 11th New York Volunteer Infantry and its twenty-four-year-old colonel, E. Elmer Ellsworth, crossed the Potomac the next day and seized Arlington, Virginia. Ellsworth entered the Marshall House Inn where a large Confederate flag was visible from the White House. Ellsworth cut down the colors— only to be fatally shot by James Jackson, the inn's owner. Sergeant Francis E. Brownell of Troy, Rensselaer County, then shot Jackson. Ellsworth would be mourned everywhere across the North as the first Union officer killed in the Civil War.

E. ELMER ELLSWORTH
Colonel 11th New York Infantry

FLAG, 11TH NEW YORK VOLUNTEER INFANTRY
Regimental flag from the 11th New York Volunteers. This regiment was raised and commanded by Elmer Ellsworth.
(New York State Military Museum, Division of Military and Naval Affairs)

ELMER ELLSWORTH
Originally from Malta, Saratoga County, Ellsworth moved to Illinois as a young man and took a job in the law office of Abraham Lincoln. Ellsworth became a tireless Lincoln supporter during the election of 1860 and accompanied him to Washington. When war broke out, Ellsworth returned to New York in order to raise a regiment.
(New York State Library, Manuscripts and Special Collections)

74

TINTYPE PORTRAIT OF ELLSWORTH
(William F. Howard Collection)

WATCH CHARM, *above right*
(New York State Museum Collection, H-1932.17.1)

SIGNATURE CARD WITH IMAGE—SERGEANT FRANCIS E. (FRANK) BROWNELL, 11TH NEW YORK STATE VOLUNTEER INFANTRY
Troy native Francis E. Brownell was celebrated as the avenger of Elmer Ellsworth and awarded the Medal of Honor.
(William F. Howard Collection)

Remember Elsworth.

PITCHER
(New York State Museum Collection, H-1973.107.2)

COMMEMORATIVE ENGRAVING
Elmer Ellsworth's death sparked an intense mourning period across the North. His body lay in state at the White House before being returned to his childhood home in Malta. Ellsworth was widely celebrated as the first martyr to the Union's cause.
(William F. Howard Collection)

Daguerreotype—Sergeant Philip R. Syland, 44th New York Volunteers
Ordnance Sergeant Philip R. Syland of Poughkeepsie, Dutchess County, from the "Ellsworth Avengers." In response to Ellsworth's murder, New York raised a unit comprised of men from each of the state's counties. *(New York State Museum Collection, H-1975.111.2)*

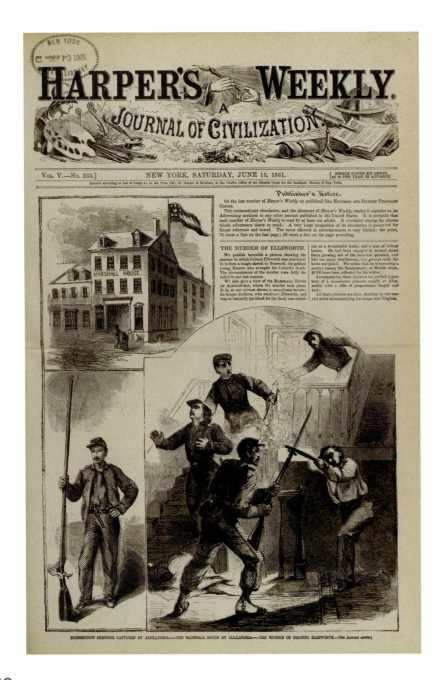

The Marshall House Flag

On April 17, 1861, just days after the Confederates bombarded Fort Sumter, James Jackson hoisted a 16 x 24 foot Confederate flag up a forty-foot flagpole atop his hotel, the Marshall House, in Alexandria, Virginia. Virginia had not yet joined other Southern states in the new Confederate States of America (a popular referendum on May 23 would decide the matter), but Jackson declared his allegiance by adorning his hotel with the Confederate flag.

THE MARSHALL HOUSE, WITH FLAG, *left*
Published in *Harper's Weekly* in June 1861, the artist depicts the Marshall House flag with eight stars, including a larger center star.
Harper's Weekly, June 15, 1861
(New York State Library, Manuscripts and Special Collections)

CURRIER & IVES, "THE DEATH OF ELLSWORTH," *right*
New York printmakers Currier & Ives captured the encounter between Colonel Ellsworth and Marshall House owner James Jackson in this 1861 lithograph. The Marshall House flag figures prominently in the artist's rendition.
(Library of Congress)

DEATH OF COL. ELLSWORTH,

after hauling down the rebel flag, at the taking of Alexandria, Va. May 24th 1861.

Marshall House Flag

The Marshall House flag conforms to the "stars and bars" pattern of the first Confederate national flag. Closely resembling the United States national flag, this flag included a blue canton with a white star for each state in the new Confederate States of America, and three stripes, or "bars," alternating red and white. Although never officially approved by the fledgling Confederate Congress, the "stars and bars" flag gained widespread acceptance and use after March 1861.
(New York State Military Museum, Division of Military and Naval Affairs)

"The Greatest Battle"
The Battle of First Bull Run, July 21, 1861

Pressured by President Lincoln and the Northern press, Union General Irvin McDowell marched toward the railroad junction at Manassas, Virginia. Of the fifty-one infantry regiments that marched with General McDowell, nineteen were from New York.

Both sides were inexperienced, but confident of an easy victory McDowell ordered an assault on Confederate positions at Bull Run Creek. Union commanders failed to coordinate assaults, instead attacking one regiment at a time. Northern troops initially drove the Confederates back, but newly arrived reinforcements blunted the attack. As more Rebel troops arrived, Union troops began a withdrawal—which turned into a rout.

THE BATTLE OF BULL RUN
The New York Times declared the Battle of Bull Run to be "The Greatest Battle Ever Fought on this Continent." Union and Confederate forces met near Manassas, Virginia. The decisive Union defeat shattered the illusion that the conflict would be short and bloodless. As the war raged, this "Greatest" of battles would be dwarfed in terms of the number of troops involved and in the horrific numbers of casualties. *Harper's Weekly,* August 10, 1861 *(New York State Library, Manuscripts and Special Collections)*

COL. MICHAEL CORCORAN, AT THE BATTLE OF BULL RUN, VA. JULY 21ST 1861.
The desperate and bloody charge of the "Gallant Sixty Ninth", on the Rebel Batteries.

COL. MICHAEL CORCORAN AT THE BATTLE OF BULL RUN, VA. JULY 21ST, 1861 BY CURRIER & IVES
The 69th Regiment, New York State Militia was heavily involved in the fighting during the Battle of Bull Run. The regiment fought bravely despite heavy casualties and served as a rear guard covering the retreat of Northern troops. The regiment's commander, Colonel Michael Corcoran

14TH REGIMENT NEW YORK STATE MILITIA, 1861–1864
Print of the 14th Regiment wearing their characteristic uniform.
(*New York State Museum Collection, H-1977.225.12*)

14th Brooklyn

Brooklyn, Kings County

When the 14th Brooklyn was passed over by New York Governor Edwin Morgan after the firing on Fort Sumter, the regiment's commander, Colonel A. M. Wood, wrote directly to Washington. The 14th was called into service by President Abraham Lincoln personally.

During the Battle of First Bull Run, the 14th distinguished itself during the fighting at Henry House Hill. Its four charges against Confederate troops led by General Thomas "Stonewall" Jackson reportedly earned the unit its nickname, the "Red Legged Devils" from the enemy commander.

During the battle, the 14th lost twenty-three men killed, sixty-four wounded, and thirty captured. Following the expiration of its nintey-day enlistment, the 14th Regiment enlisted en masse as the 84th New York Volunteers, though it continued to be called the 14th Brooklyn.

"Hold on, Boys! Here come those
Red Legged Devils again."
—*Confederate General Thomas
"Stonewall" Jackson to his men
during the Battle of First Bull Run,
July 21, 1861*

14TH BROOKLYN AT FIRST BULL RUN, *right*
(*New York State Military Museum, Division of Military and Naval Affairs*)

CHASSEUR TUNIC, TROUSERS, GAITERS, AND KEPI

The 14th Regiment, New York State Militia, was organized in July 1847 in Brooklyn. In 1860, following a performance of Elmer Ellsworth's United States Zouave Cadets, the officers of the 14th adopted a French-style chasseur uniform with distinctive red trousers. While most units in the Union Army adopted a navy blue sack coat and sky blue trousers, the City of Brooklyn paid to allow the 14th regiment to maintain this uniform throughout the Civil War. The white gaiters feature seven gold buttons on each leg, representing the 14th Regiment. *(New York State Military Museum, Division of Military and Naval Affairs)*

RETURN OF THE 69TH, *right*

This *Harper's Weekly* illustration depicts the return of the 69th Regiment, New York State Militia, to New York City after the Battle of Bull Run. With the end of their ninety-day enlistment, the regiment returned to state control. Many members of the unit volunteered to serve for three additional years in the 69th New York Volunteer Infantry Regiment. *(The Myer Family)*

From Ninety Days to Three Years

Following the disastrous defeat at Bull Run, the North began to come to terms with the prospect of a lengthy war to suppress the rebellion. On July 22, 1861, President Lincoln issued a new call for 500,000 volunteers to serve three-year enlistments. In New York, Governor Morgan oversaw the return of the ninety-day militia volunteers while also organizing the new three-year regiments that needed to be armed, equipped, and sent to Washington. By the end of July, Congress authorized all new volunteer regiments to serve for the duration of the war.

RECEPTION BY THE PEOPLE OF NEW YORK OF THE SIXTY-NINTH REGIMENT, N. Y. S. M., ON THEIR RETURN FROM THE SEAT OF WAR, ESCORTED BY THE NEW YORK SEVENTH REGIMENT.

The return home of the gallant Sixty-ninth Regiment—composed entirely of Irish citizens—on Saturday, July 27th, 1861, was an ovation as warm and enthusiastic as their endurance and bravery deserved. Their service of three months had been of infinite value to their country and honor to themselves and their State. The Sixty-ninth had rendered good service at Arlington Heights, and especially distinguished itself at the battle of Bull Run. On the morning of their arrival the streets were crowded with people, and the gallant fellows were greeted with shouts of applause along the whole line of march.

Chester A. Arthur

As New York prepared to send troops to war, the government struggled to develop an effective means to arm and equip the large numbers of volunteers. Governor Morgan appointed Chester A. Arthur as State Quartermaster General. Arthur proved highly adept at organizing the vast logistics necessary for an uninterrupted flow of materials to New York's troops in the field.

CHESTER A. ARTHUR
A beneficiary of Governor Edwin Morgan's patronage, Chester Arthur rose through the ranks of New York's Republican Party. Despite his exemplary record, Arthur was relieved as Quartermaster in 1863 following the election of Democrat Horatio Seymour. Arthur remained active in politics and became President of the United States in 1881, following the assassination of James Garfield.
(Library of Congress)

Clothing the Troops
New York's Textile Industry

The outbreak of war ended the importation of cotton from the South. Government money, however, enabled New York's textile mills to retool in order to produce inexpensive wool clothing for the U.S. Army. During the war, production in New York's cotton mills declined, but the manufacture of woolen goods increased dramatically.

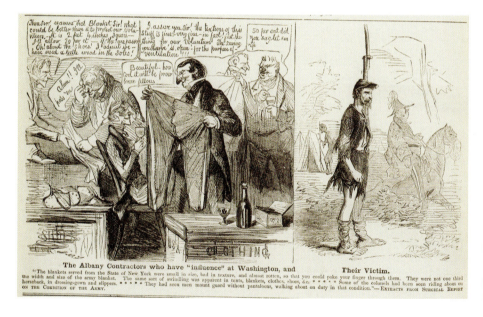

The Albany Contractors who have "influence" at Washington, and   Their Victim.

"The blankets served from the State of New York were small in size, bad in texture, and almost rotten, so that you could poke your finger through them. They were not one third the width and size of the army blanket. The same sort of swindling was apparent in tents, blankets, clothes, shoes, &c. * * * * Some of the colonels had been seen riding about on horseback, in dressing-gown and slippers. * * * * They had seen men mount guard without pantaloons, walking about on duty in that condition."—EXTRACTS FROM SURGICAL REPORT ON THE CONDITION OF THE ARMY.

THE ALBANY CONTRACTORS . . .
As New York industry mobilized for the war effort, some businessmen could not resist the temptation to profit from the conflict, as suggested in this August 10, 1861 *Harper's Weekly* cartoon.
(New York State Library, Manuscripts and Special Collections)

FELT HAT
New York's textile manufacturers capitalized on new opportunities to produce uniforms for the growing Union Army. This brimmed hat was made by the Samuel Stocking Company of Utica, Oneida County.
(New York State Museum Collection, H-1947.4.7)

NEW YORK PATTERN JACKET
State Militia regulations authorized the New York Pattern wool uniform coat for issue to all state regiments in April 1861. The coat would eventually be issued to more than one hundred volunteer regiments.
(New York State Military Museum, Division of Military and Naval Affairs)

Arming the War Effort

New York's Firearms Industry

New York State gunsmiths dominated the industry throughout the first half of the nineteenth century. As the Civil War raged, demand from state and federal government contracts strained even the most established arms makers. The technology of war progressed rapidly as smooth-bore flintlock muskets were replaced by rifled guns with percussion cap firing mechanisms. Eventually, the introduction of metallic cartridges signaled the end of the muzzle-loading era. New York's firearms industry equipped Union soldiers with these new and emerging technologies.

REMINGTON CONVERSION MUSKET—E. REMINGTON & SONS (ILION)
At the start of the war, demand for firearms rapidly outpaced production capacity. This Remington flintlock musket was converted to a percussion cap firing system. The holes for the flint lock remain visible. The percussion cap, made of brass or copper, contained a small amount of priming powder that sparked and ignited when the trigger was pulled. This advancement enabled the weapon to be fired in all weather. *(New York State Museum Collection, H-1970.30.2)*

PERCUSSION RIFLE (1850s)—PATRICK SMITH (BUFFALO)
By the mid-1840s, Irish-born Patrick Smith had established himself as the leading gunsmith in Buffalo, Erie County, producing hunting and fowling rifles. During the war, Smith produced rifles for Buffalo-area regiments. *(New York State Museum Collection, H-1993.12.1)*

CARBINE—STARR ARMS COMPANY (YONKERS)
In addition to revolvers, the Starr Arms Company also produced carbines, including more than 20,000 of this .54 caliber, breech-loading variety. Carbines were shorter than infantry rifles and were preferred by cavalry units attempting to fight on horseback. Breech loading was faster than muzzle loading and allowed cavalry troopers to fire more rapidly than their infantry counterparts. The shorter barrels, however, decreased the weapon's range. *(New York State Museum Collection, H-1942.5.12)*

RIFLE SCOPE—MALCOLM RIFLE TELESCOPE COMPANY (SYRACUSE)
Around 1840, target shooters began to put telescopic sights on their rifles to improve accuracy. The Army adopted the devices for use by its sharpshooters during the Civil War. This scope was constructed by the Malcolm Rifle Telescope Manufacturing Company of Syracuse. New York State was the largest producer of rifle telescopes until the 1890s.
(Onondaga Historical Association)

SPRINGFIELD CONTRACT RIFLE—E. ROBINSON (NEW YORK CITY)
This M1861 Springfield Rifle Musket was produced under government contract by E. Robinson in New York City. To meet the growing demand for weapons, the U.S. Army's Springfield Armory issued contracts to manufacturers throughout the North for the Model 1861. By the war's end, E. Robinson had delivered thirty thousand of the firearms to the Union Army.
(New York State Museum Collection, H-1971.91.2 A-C)

SPRINGFIELD CONTRACT RIFLE—UNION ARMS COMPANY (NEW YORK CITY)
Union Arms Company in New York City produced nearly three hundred M1861s in addition to other weapons for the Union war effort.
(New York State Museum Collection, H1971.91.1)

REMINGTON REVOLVER—E. REMINGTON & SONS (UTICA)
During the Civil War, Remington Arms Company became the second largest (after Colt) supplier of revolvers to the Union Army. Located along the Erie Canal in Ilion, Herkimer County, the company constructed a second factory at Utica, Oneida County, devoted solely to the manufacture of pistols. By the end of the war, Remington Arms had earned nearly three million dollars supplying weapons for the North.
(New York State Museum Collection, H-XX.279.1)

REVOLVER—STARR ARMS COMPANY (YONKERS)
With factories in Yonkers and Binghamton, the Starr Arms Company was the third largest supplier of revolvers to the Union Army during the Civil War. By the war's end, the company had delivered 47,952 revolvers to the Federal Government.
(New York State Museum Collection, H-1968.66.5)

Financing the War Effort

The Civil War required government expenditures on an unprecedented scale. Federal and state treasuries were stretched. Wall Street played a crucial role in financing the Northern war effort. New York banks readily lent money to the U.S. and state governments for the arming and equipping of troops.

Businessmen of both political parties voted to establish the Union Defense Committee to donate personal fortunes to the war effort. Further, following the passage of the Revenue Act in July 1862, New Yorkers provided more money in income taxes than any other state.

THE GOLD AND STOCK EXCHANGE
Drawing depicting large crowds awaiting the opening of New York City markets. Wall Street was instrumental in financing the war effort. *New York Illustrated News,* October 25, 1862 *(New York State Library, Manuscripts and Special Collections)*

THE GOLD AND STOCK EXCITEMENT—CROWD OF BULLS AND BEARS ON WILLIAM STREET, NEAR EXCHANGE PLACE, BEFORE THE MEETING OF THE FIRST BOARD OF BROKERS. SEE PAGE 387.

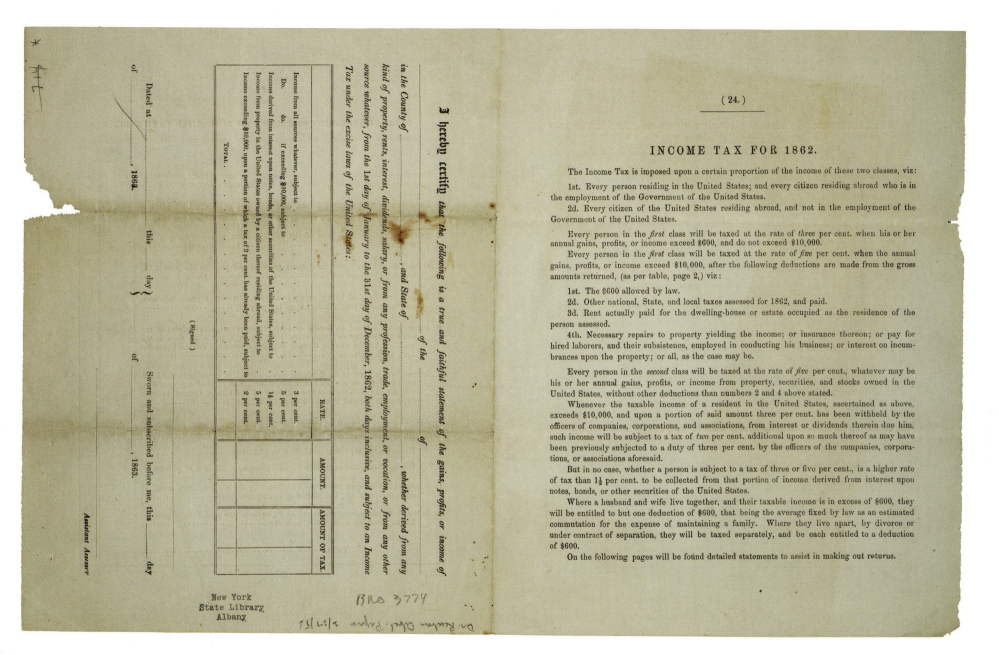

Broadside

To finance the war, the Revenue Act established a 3 percent tax on incomes over $800. The tax was not repealed until 1872. *(New York State Library, Manuscripts and Special Collections)*

CERTIFICATE
Local and county governments
frequently offered bounty
payments to entice soldiers to
volunteer for service. A $100
bounty would be worth over
two thousand dollars today.
Sometimes these bounties were
paid by the state; at other times
local individuals or groups
provided the funding.
*(New York State Museum
Collection, H-1976.46.2)*

RECEIPT BOOK
Receipt ledger from
Brookhaven, Suffolk County,
indicating bounty paid to each
volunteer.
*(Courtesy of Barbara Russell,
Brookhaven Town Historian)*

STATE OF NEW-YORK.

Paymaster General's Office,

Albany, *Aug 2* 1862.

Hon. LUCIUS ROBINSON, Comptroller.

Sir:—I require for the payment of Bounties to soldiers mustered into the United States service, in accordance with the Proclamation of His Excellency, Edwin D. Morgan, Governor, dated July 17, 1862, the sum of *Twenty thousand* Dollars.

Your Obedient Servant,

APPROVED *Aug 2 1862*

E. D. Morgan

Paymaster General.

TREASURER'S OFFICE,
STATE OF NEW-YORK.

Received from WILLIAM B. LEWIS, Treasurer of this State, *twenty thousand* Dollars, in full of the annexed Warrant.

Albany, 186

$

The following inquiries are submitted through the Superintendent of the Banking Department to the Officers of the .... *Seamen Bank for* Savings, ~~Bank~~ located at *New York City.* By the Chief of the Bureau of Military Statistics.

I. About what amount of money has been deposited in your Bank, by Soldiers directly, either through the Allotment system or otherwise? *$278.08*

II. About what proportion of the deposits made in your Bank during the year ending with July 1, 1864, were by Soldiers or members of Soldiers' families? *Small—say 2½ per Cent*

III. Were any considerable number of these Soldiers or Soldiers' families depositors in your Bank before the commencement of the present war? *Very few*

IV. Any fact connected with loaning money by your Bank for war purposes, or other fact of interest connected with the war, would be thankfully received. *This Bank has virtually loaned to various States of the Union, by taking of their Stocks, issued for war purposes, directly from the State Authorities, one million five hundred thousand dollars*

Please Sign here Officially.

E. Platt Cashier

Dated at *New York*

August 5 1864

LOAN VOUCHERS
Banks and financial institutions across the state began loaning large sums of money to finance the war effort. *(New York State Archives)*

Twelfth President of New York Historical Society, 1867–1869.

HAMILTON FISH
Former New York governor Hamilton Fish was appointed the chairman of the Union Defense Committee.
(New York State Library, Manuscripts and Special Collections)

Union Defense Committee

Businessmen of both political parties voted to establish the Union Defense Committee (UDC) to raise funds to support the arming and equipping of New York's soldiers. The committee raised millions of dollars in response to President Lincoln's call to arms. By the end of 1861, the UDC had helped to raise and equip sixty-six regiments for the Union Army.

The UDC and Governor Morgan clashed over responsibility for raising volunteers. Telegraphing a complaint directly to President Lincoln, Morgan argued that he alone had the authority to dispatch troops. Eventually, all of New York's regiments were placed under Morgan's command until entering federal service.

Watervliet Arsenal, Watervliet, Albany County

Watervliet Arsenal was established in 1813 to supply troops along the northern frontier during the War of 1812. Employing nearly two thousand workers during the Civil War, Watervliet Arsenal produced a variety of goods for the Union war effort.

SHIPMENT OF GUNS AND AMMUNITION FROM THE WATERVLIET ARSENAL, TROY, N.Y., *top right*
Frank Leslie's Illustrated print depicting war matériel being loaded aboard vessels on the Erie Canal.
(New York State Library, Manuscripts and Special Collections)

RIFLE SLING, ARTILLERY VALISE, HORSE BIT, ARTILLERY VENT PUNCHES, *bottom right*
Watervliet Arsenal was a major supplier of leather accoutrements, paper cartridges, and artillery equipment to the Union Army.
(New York State Museum Collection, H-1970.21.1, H-XX.324.1, H-1976.191.3, H-1975.174.3–.4)

95

New York's Iron Industry

New York's foundries manufactured iron at an unprecedented rate during the war and provided the U.S. with a wide array of essential materials. By the mid-nineteenth century, the state was one of the nation's leading producers of pig and cast iron, and Essex County mines were the country's second-leading source of iron ore.

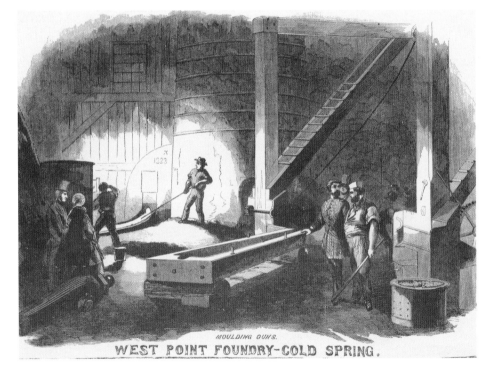

MOLDING CANNONS AT THE WEST POINT FOUNDRY
New York's iron industry played a crucial part in arming the North's armies for what was to become a long and deadly conflict.
Harper's Weekly, September 14, 1861
(New York State Library, Manuscripts and Special Collections)

BROADSIDE, STARBUCK BROTHERS, TROY, RENSSELAER COUNTY
New York's iron industry quickly transitioned to the manufacture of war materials.
(New York State Library, Manuscripts and Special Collections)

J. L. Mott Iron Works, Westchester County

By the Civil War, the J. L. Mott Iron Works employed nearly two hundred men and was one of the largest in the country. It manufactured stoves, pipes, plumber castings, and more. The company transitioned to the manufacture of war material during the war. *New York Illustrated News,* September 26, 1863. *(New York State Library, Manuscripts and Special)*

Burden Iron Works, Troy, Rensselaer County

Established by Scottish immigrant Henry Burden in the 1820s, the Burden Iron Works was situated along the Wynantskill near the banks of the Hudson River. Utilizing this abundant water power, Burden constructed the most powerful water wheel in the world in 1851.

Burden was a prolific inventor. His inventions included machines to mass produce horseshoes and hook-headed railroad spikes. During the Civil War, the Burden factories employed 1,400 workers manufacturing horseshoes, rivets, bolts, and other materials for the Northern war effort.

HENRY BURDEN
Scottish immigrant Henry Burden arrived in Troy in 1822. Burden invented a machine that enabled him to mass produce iron horseshoes.
(History of Rensselaer Co., New York, by Nathaniel Bartlett Sylvester, 1880)

BURDEN HORSESHOE
A Civil War–era Burden horseshoe. The Burden Iron Works manufactured nearly all of the horseshoes used by the Union Army during the war.
(Hudson Mohawk Industrial Gateway)

MODEL, HORSESHOE MACHINE
This model of Henry Burden's horseshoe machine was constructed for a display on American innovation at the Centennial Exposition in Philadelphia, Pennsylvania, in 1876.
(New York State Museum Collection, H-1946.6.1)

KEG
Burden's horseshoes were delivered to Army ferriers in 100 lb. kegs. At the peak of production, Burden Iron Works was producing 600,000 kegs of horseshoes annually.
(Hudson Mohawk Industrial Gateway)

Burden's Horse-Shoe Machine.

BURDEN'S HORSESHOE MACHINE
Henry Burden's horseshoe machine was capable of producing sixty horseshoes per minute,
or up to fifty million per year. *(New York State Museum Collection, 1940.19.1)*

The Parrott Gun and the West Point Foundry, Cold Spring, Putnam County

Established in 1817, the West Point Foundry was one of the nation's oldest by 1861. Foundry superintendent Robert Parker

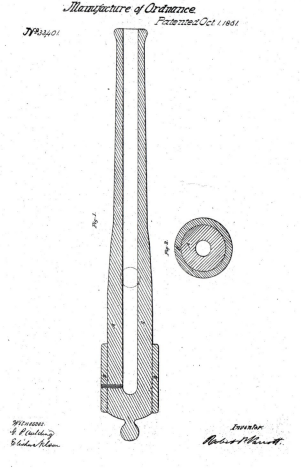

Parrott patented its most notable product, the Parrott Rifled Cannon, in 1861. The Parrott Gun was more accurate than smooth-bore cannons and could be produced cheaper than other rifled designs. The West Point Foundry's 1,400 workers supplied the U.S. war effort with two thousand cannons and three million artillery shells.

PARROTT GUNS OF THE 1ST INDEPENDENT BATTERY, NEW YORK VOLUNTEERS, *right*
Photograph depicting the Parrott Guns of the 1st Independent Battery, New York Volunteers, in the spring of 1862. Even early in the war, New York's industrial might was demonstrably visible on the battlefield.
(Library of Congress)

PATENT DRAWING
Robert Parrott's patent drawing for his new artillery pieces.
(New York State Library, Manuscripts and Special Collections)

PARROTT GUN
Parrott's rifled cannons were produced by casting the guns around a hollow core. This allowed the tube to cool from inside as well as out. The breech end of the cannon was then bound with a red-hot iron band that shrank as it cooled to create a tight fit. This strengthened the cannon's breech and allowed more powder to be used, thereby increasing the gun's power and range.
(New York State Military Museum, Division of Military and Naval Affairs)

New York's Shipbuilding Industry

The Civil War marked a transition in naval warfare—from wooden sailing and steam ships to heavily armored ironclads. Congress ordered the study of iron-plated warships in July 1861. But with news that the Confederate Navy was working on its own ironclad, production was rushed ahead at the Continental Iron Works at Greenpoint, Long Island. The government issued contracts for iron plating to numerous firms, including the Troy Iron Works. Once construction of the U.S.S. *Monitor* was completed, the ship was outfitted and equipped at the Brooklyn Navy Yard.

New York State's many shipyards and maritime industries contributed significantly to the war effort. They enabled the expansion of the American Navy and the construction of the newest steam-powered warships and ironclad vessels. Most of these companies were located in New York City—the nation's leading port—and the Hudson Valley.

BROOKLYN NAVY YARD
Established in 1800 as the U.S. Naval Shipyard, New York, the Brooklyn Navy Yard played an especially pivotal role in arming and equipping the American fleet. Workers at the yard constructed sixteen warships—and in 1862 outfitted the Union ironclad, U.S.S. *Monitor.*
Harper's Weekly, August 24, 1861
(New York State Library, Manuscripts and Special Collections)

102

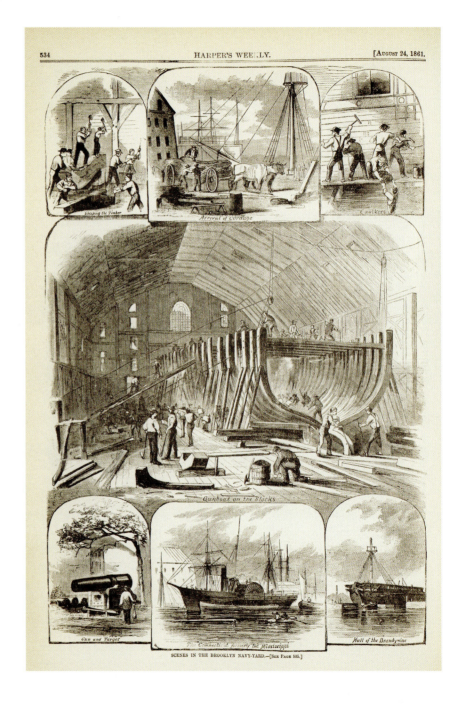

U.S.S. *Passaic* testing her guns in the Palisades
New York shipyards were instrumental in the development of the U.S. Navy's new ironclad warships. With many of these yards located in the Lower Hudson Valley, the Hudson Highlands provided the Navy with ample space to test fire the ships' new weaponry. In 2007, wildfires in the region caused unexploded ordnance from these tests to explode, adding to the dangers posed by the fires. *Harper's Weekly*, November 29, 1862 *(New York State Library, Manuscripts and Special Collections)*

HARPER'S NEW MONTHLY MAGAZINE.

No. CXLVIII.—SEPTEMBER, 1862.—Vol. XXV.

LAUNCH OF THE "MONITOR."

IRON-CLAD VESSELS.

ON the 16th of September, 1861, the Committee of Naval Constructors appointed to examine the various plans presented for the building of iron-clad vessels made their report to the Secretary of the Navy. Plans and specifications were submitted to them for vessels ranging from 83 to 400 feet in length, to cost from $32,000 to $1,500,000. Of these they recommended three for adoption: the *Galena*; the *Ironsides*, now building at Philadelphia; and Mr. Ericsson's *Monitor*. Their approval of the *Monitor* was cautiously worded. They say:

"This is novel, but seems to be based upon a plan which will render the battery shot and shell proof. We are somewhat apprehensive that her properties for sea are not such as a sea-going vessel should possess. But she may be moved from place to place on our coast in smooth water. We recommend that an experiment be made with one battery of this description on the terms proposed, with a guaranty and forfeiture in case of a failure in any of the points and properties of the vessel as proposed."

This Committee could not have anticipated

Vol. XXV.—No. 148.—E e

Clash of the Ironclads

U.S.S. *Monitor* vs. C.S.S. *Virginia*

President Lincoln ordered the U.S. Navy to blockade the Confederacy in order to cut off the rebellious states from supplies and vital trade that could fund their war effort. The Navy hastily assembled and armed two hundred ships of all types by the end of the year. As the war progressed, the increased size of the U.S. Navy made a more effective blockade.

On March 8, 1862, the C.S.S. *Virginia* (rebuilt from the U.S.S. *Merrimac*) sailed out of Norfolk, Virginia, to confront the blockading Union ships. In a few short hours, the *Virginia* had sunk two of the North's most formidable warships. The battle showed the inability of wooden-hulled ships to fare against the new ironclads. That night, the U.S.S. *Monitor*, which had been rushed from New York Harbor, arrived at Hampton Roads.

THE LAUNCHING OF THE U.S.S. *Monitor*
Harper's Monthly Magazine drawing of the *Monitor's* launch from the Continental Iron Works, January 30, 1862.
(New York State Library, Manuscripts and Special Collections)

ENGAGEMENT BETWEEN THE *Monitor* AND THE *Merrimac*
On March 9, the first ever battle between two ironclad ships ended in an indecisive draw. While the *Virginia* safely returned to Norfolk, the *Monitor* had succeeded in preventing the destruction of the entire Union blockading squadron. *(New York State Archives)*

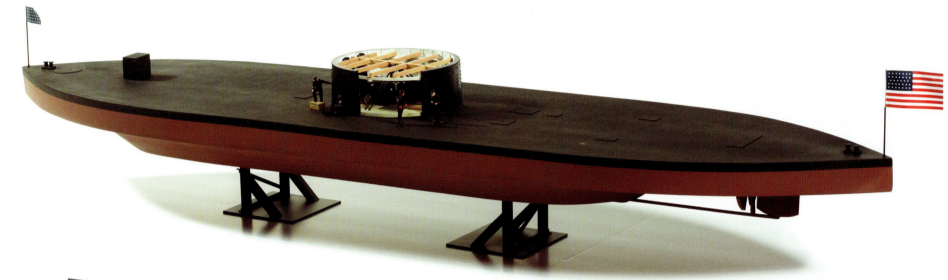

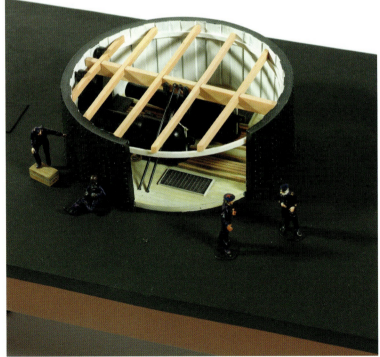

U.S.S. *Monitor, above and left*
After its battle with the *Virginia,* the *Monitor* remained with the Atlantic Blockade Fleet. The ship sank in a storm off Cape Hatteras, North Carolina, on December 31, 1862. Despite her short service, the *Monitor* revolutionized naval shipbuilding forever.
(Robert Keough, U.S. Naval Landing Party)

Iron Plate, *near right*
This iron plate was reportedly rolled for the U.S.S. *Monitor* at the Corning & Winslow foundry in Troy, Rensselaer County. The piece, likely part of the ship's hull plating, was never used and, in 1980, was found in a vault of the Portec Rail Company (a descendant of Corning and Winslow). *(Hudson Mohawk Industrial Gateway)*

The Ericsson Steel–Plated Battery, *far right*
Newspapers described John Ericsson's new warship as "a revolving fort" that was "one of the most novel and interesting pieces of naval architecture [ever] constructed." *Harper's Weekly,* December 21, 1861 *(New York State Library, Manuscripts and Special Collections)*

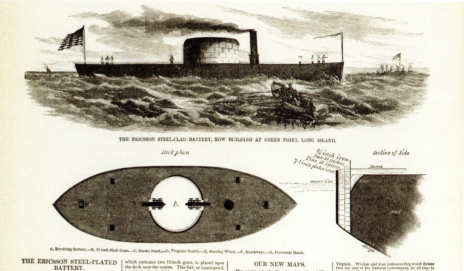

THE ERICSSON STEEL-CLAD BATTERY, NOW BUILDING AT GREEN POINT, LONG ISLAND.

Deck plan   *Section of Side*

A, Revolving Battery.—B, 12-inch Shell Guns.—C, Smoke Stack.—D, Propeller Scuttle.—E, Steering Wheel.—F, Hatchways.—G, Forecastle Hatch.

THE ERICSSON STEEL-PLATED BATTERY.

THE ERICSSON BATTERY, a sketch of which will be found on this page, is now in process of construction at the Continental Iron Works at Green Point, Long Island. She will be launched in the course of a few days. She is about 200 feet in length, with 36 feet beam and 11 feet depth of hold. Her hull is built of iron, and to protect her sides she is covered with a layer of oak 14 inches in thickness, another layer of pine 14 inches in thickness, the whole being plated with seven plates of one inch iron, making her shot-proof. A revolving fort, which contains two 12-inch guns, is placed upon the deck near the centre. This fort, or bomb-proof, is eight inches in thickness. The diameter of the fort is 20 feet inside, and it is 10 feet in height. She will be propelled by a powerful Ericsson engine. She is one of the most novel and interesting pieces of naval architecture constructed in this country. For proper reasons we forbear to give very full details in relation to this vessel, as we do not desire to give the rebels any information on such matters.

Other iron-clad vessels are being built at Philadelphia, Pennsylvania, and Mystic, Connecticut. By next summer we shall have several afloat.

OUR NEW MAPS.

WE continue in this Number the series of WAR MAPS, which have been so marked a feature of this journal since the war began. On this page we give a map showing the proposed reconstruction of the States of Virginia, Maryland, and Delaware. This can be best understood by reference to the following extract from the Report of the Secretary of War:

The geographical position of the metropolis of the nation, menaced by the rebels, and required to be defended by thousands of our troops, induces me to suggest for consideration the propriety and expediency of a reconstruction of the boundaries of the States of Delaware, Maryland, and

Virginia. Wisdom and true statesmanship would dictate that the seat of the National Government, for all time to come, should be placed beyond reasonable danger of seizure by enemies within, as well as from capture by foes from without. By agreement between the states named, such as war effected, for similar purposes, by Michigan and Ohio, and by Missouri and Iowa, their boundaries could be so changed as to render the capital more remote than at present from the influence of State governments which have arrayed themselves in rebellion against the Federal authority. To this end, the limits of Virginia might be so altered as to make her boundaries consist of the Blue Ridge on the east and Pennsylvania on the north, leaving those on the south and west as at present. By the arrangement two counties of Maryland (Alleghany and Washington) would be transferred to the jurisdiction of Virginia. All that portion of Virginia which lies between the Blue Ridge and Chesapeake Bay could then be added to Maryland, while

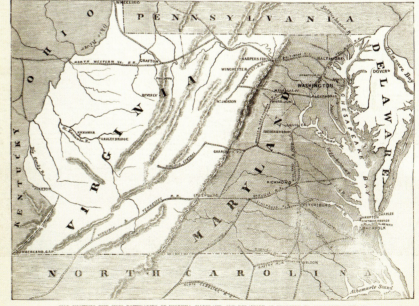

MAP SHOWING THE NEW BOUNDARIES OF VIRGINIA, MARYLAND, AND DELAWARE AS PROPOSED BY SECRETARY CAMERON.

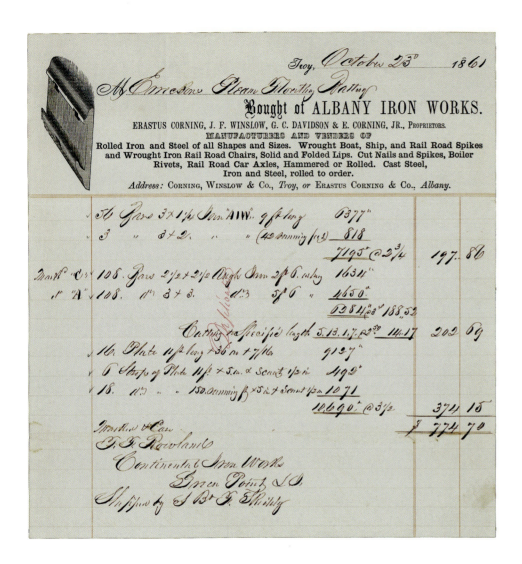

JOHN ERICSSON
Engineer

ACCOUNTING, ERICSSON'S STEAM FLOATING BATTERY
Account ledgers and receipts from the Albany Iron Works, one of several companies contracted for the construction of the U.S.S. *Monitor*.
(New York State Library, Manuscripts and Special Collections)

JOHN ERICSSON
Swedish-born engineer John Ericsson revolutionized naval warfare with his invention of the U.S.S. *Monitor*.
(New York State Library, Manuscripts and Special Collections)

Redefining the War (1862–1863)

As the war entered its second year, both sides gained combat experience and developed new, skilled leaders. Casualties rose even as battles remained indecisive. Confederates shifted from their defensive strategy and invaded Maryland, hoping to turn public sentiment against the war effort.

Initially, President Lincoln insisted that restoring the Union was the war's only purpose and made no immediate move to end slavery, since he believed that most Northerners would not support emancipation. As the war dragged on, however, Lincoln decided the time had come to initiate an emancipation policy.

The Emancipation Proclamation made the Civil War a crusade for abolition as well as for the preservation of the Union. New Yorkers responded differently to the proclamation when it took effect on January 1, 1863. Implementation of the proclamation required success on the battlefield, however, and this was by no means assured in early 1863.

FLAG, IV CORPS, ARMY OF THE POTOMAC
This flag belonged to Albany's Lieutenant Colonel John G. Farnsworth, Assistant Quartermaster of IV Corps, and flew over its headquarters during McClellan's Peninsula Campaign.
(New York State Museum Collection, H-1952.7.5)

The Road to Emancipation

The Peninsula Campaign and Antietam

In an effort to capture the Confederate capital at Richmond, Virginia, General George B. McClellan launched a campaign along the peninsula between the York and James Rivers even as Confederate forces in the Shenandoah Valley threatened Washington, D.C. After a series of defeats, McClellan returned to Washington.

During the summer of 1862, President Lincoln raised the idea of emancipating Southern slaves. With McClellan's failure on the peninsula, Secretary of State William Seward urged the president to wait for a Union victory in order to issue such a proclamation from a position of strength.

Battle of Antietam, September 17, 1862

The Battle of Antietam was the bloodiest day of battle in the entire Civil War. New Yorkers—who comprised approximately 20 percent of the Army of the Potomac—were in the thick of a fight that resulted in 23,000 total casualties.

Fought near Antietam Creek, Maryland, this was the first major battle to take place on Union soil. There was no clear-cut victory for either the United States or the Confederacy, but Antietam ended Confederate General Robert E. Lee's first invasion of the North. Lee's withdrawal to Virginia would provide Lincoln with the opportunity to issue his Preliminary Emancipation Proclamation.

SWORD
This sword belonged to Lieutenant Colonel John G. Wright of the 51st New York.
(*William F. Howard Collection*)

BATTLE OF FAIR OAKS
This image shows the charge of the 69th and 88th Regiments, New York Volunteers, during the Battle of Fair Oaks, Virginia.
(*New York State Library, Manuscripts and Special Collections*)

PHOTOGRAPH OF THE DEAD AT SUNKEN ROAD
The introduction of photography drastically altered public perception of the conflict. For the first time, people were confronted by the horrors of battle. This image of the Sunken Road at Antietam—where 1,750 Union soldiers fell in less than one hour—was one of many taken following the bloodiest day of the war. *(Library of Congress)*

51ST NEW YORK AND 51ST PENNSYLVANIA CHARGE ACROSS BURNSIDE'S BRIDGE
This *Frank Leslie's Illustrated* print depicts one of Antietam's bloodiest scenes, as Union troops, including the 51st New York, attempted to fight their way across Antietam Creek. *(New York State Library, Manuscripts and Special Collections)*

60th New York Volunteer Infantry

Organized at Ogdensburg, St. Lawrence County, in October 1861, the 60th Regiment, New York Volunteers, distinguished itself during the Battle of Antietam. The regiment was assigned to 2nd Division, XII Corps. When 1st Division failed to break through Rebel defenses and push toward Dunker Church, the 60th moved to cover the Corps' exposed flank. During fighting in the West Woods, twenty men were killed, wounded, or captured.

DRUM
Snare drum used by Private Joseph Lyons of the 60th New York Volunteer Infantry. Lyons survived the war and became a successful businessman in Ogdensburg.
(St. Lawrence County Historical Association)

PORTRAIT OF PRIVATE JOSEPH LYONS
(St. Lawrence County Historical Association)

Published by Chas Magnus.   Advance Guard Cavalry — near Alexandria, Va.   12 Frankfort St. N.Y.

THE DRUMMER OF ANTIETAM,

Air : Last Rose of Summer. — By Eugene Johnston.

The drummer of Antietam,
  Lays dead and alone ;
Upon the cold battle field,
  Where his blood hath flown
No friends mourn around him,
  No comrades are near.
To lament his early fate,
  Or o'er him shed a tear.

Now the moon faintly beams,
  On the spot where he lays ;
Making his features more ghastly,
  With its misty rays ;
While hundreds sleep near him,
  In deaths icy chain ;
Who've fought their last battle,
  Who'll ne'er wake again.

And thus are the bravest,
  Cut off in their bloom,
And manhoods hopes crushed
  In the cold tomb ;
But they shall be cherished,
  In ths hearts of the free,
As true martyrs of justice,
  And sweet Liberty.

500 Illustrated Ballads, lithographed and printed by
CHARLES MAGNUS, No. 12 Frankfort Street, New York.
Branch Office : No. 520 7th St. Washington, D. C.

BD 1414

Brigadier General Max Weber

A former German military officer, Max Weber emigrated to the United States with other revolutionaries in 1849 and settled in New York City. With the outbreak of war, Weber joined the Union Army. He served during the Peninsula Campaign in Virginia. Promoted to brigadier general, Weber commanded a brigade at Antietam. As part of II Corps, Weber's men were ordered to attack a strong Rebel position along a Sunken Road at the center of the battlefield. Almost immediately, Weber fell, his right arm badly wounded in the attack.

BROADSIDE BALLAD, *The Drummer of Antietam*
Broadside ballads were one good way of disseminating news throughout the war. These ballads often covered the important issues and events of the day with editorial slants, making them a mirror of societal opinions of their time. As the lists of casualties mounted— and particularly after Antietam, the bloodiest single day of the war— the public began to change its perceptions of the conflict.
(New York State Library, Manuscripts and Special Collections)

BRIGADIER GENERAL MAX WEBER, *(right)*
Max Weber enlisted to fight in the Civil War as a colonel on May 16, 1861. He raised a German American unit known as the Turner Rifles, a company that eventually became a part of the 20th New York Infantry. Due to the severity of his wounds from Antietam, Weber was never again able to command troops in the field. He served the remainder of the war in an administrative role in the capital.
(New York State Museum Collection, H-1984.85.7)

BINOCULARS, COLT REVOLVER, AND SWORD
CARRIED BY GENERAL MAX WEBER DURING THE WAR
(New York State Museum Collection, H-1984.85.2)

The Preliminary Emancipation Proclamation

President Lincoln changed the meaning of the war on September 22, 1862. The Battle of Antietam provided him with the victory he had been waiting for. Citing his power as commander in chief, Lincoln issued his Preliminary Emancipation Proclamation as a military order. It declared that in one hundred days the federal government would deem all slaves within Rebel territory to be "forever" free on January 1, 1863, unless the Confederate states returned to the Union. The revolutionary document began the process of making abolition the central goal of the war.

Lincoln crafted this document carefully. It did not immediately abolish slavery everywhere in the United States—only in the regions not under Union control. By making the war a crusade against slavery, Lincoln improved U.S. relations abroad and weakened the Confederacy economically.

The Preliminary Emancipation Proclamation is the only surviving Proclamation document in Lincoln's own hand. Lincoln probably glued in sections of the Congressional Confiscation Act to save time—the fingerprint visible on the first page of the document is probably his own. In 1864, Lincoln donated the document to the U.S. Sanitary Commission, which raffled it off at the Albany Relief Bazaar to help raise money for the Union war effort. Abolitionist Gerrit Smith won the raffle after buying one thousand tickets at $1 apiece. Smith then sold the document to the New York State Legislature, with funds going to the Sanitary Commission. The legislature, in turn, deposited the document in the New York State Library, where it remains today.

STAMPEDE OF SLAVES
Slaves had long attempted to escape to Union lines when Northern armies were nearby. After the Emancipation Proclamation, slaves arriving in Union camps were considered free individuals, not just "contraband property." *Harper's Weekly*, January 31, 1863 *(New York State Library, Manuscripts and Special Collections)*

"First Reading of the Emancipation Proclamation by Abraham Lincoln" (1864), by Francis Bicknell Carpenter
This print of Lincoln reading his Emancipation Proclamation to his cabinet was created by Francis Bicknell Carpenter of Homer, Cortland County. Pictured from left to right are Secretary of War Edwin M. Stanton, Secretary of the Treasury Salmon P. Chase, President Lincoln, Secretary of the Navy Gideon Welles, Secretary of the Interior Caleb Blood Smith, Secretary of State William H. Seward, Postmaster General Montgomery Blair, and Attorney General Edward Bates. *(National Archives and Records Administration)*

I, Abraham Lincoln, President of the United States of America, and Commander-in-Chief of the Army and Navy thereof, do hereby proclaim and declare that hereafter, as heretofore, the war will be prosecuted for the object of practically restoring the constitutional relation between the United States, and each of the states, and the people thereof, in which states that relation is, or may be suspended, or disturbed.

That it is my purpose, upon the next meeting of Congress to again recommend the adoption of a practical measure tendering pecuniary aid to the free acceptance or rejection of all slave-states, so called, the people whereof may not then be in rebellion against the United States, and which states may then have voluntarily adopted, or thereafter may voluntarily adopt, immediate, or gradual abolishment of slavery within their respective limits; and that the effort to colonize persons of African descent upon this continent, or elsewhere, will be continued.

That on the first day of January in the year of our Lord, one thousand eight hundred and sixty-three, all persons held as slaves within any state, or designated part of a state, the people whereof shall then be in rebellion against the United States, shall be then, thenceforward, and forever free; and the executive government of the United States, including the military and naval authority thereof, will recognize and maintain the freedom of such persons, and will do no act or acts to repress such persons, or any of them, in any efforts they may make for their actual freedom.

That the executive will, on the first day of January aforesaid, by proclamation, designate the states, and parts of states, if any, in which the people thereof respectively, shall then be in rebellion against the United States; and the fact that any state, or the people thereof shall, on that day be, in good faith represented in the Congress of the United States, by members chosen thereto, at elections wherein a majority of the

THE FOUR-PAGE DRAFT OF THE PRELIMINARY EMANCIPATION PROCLAMATION, WRITTEN IN LINCOLN'S HANDWRITING. *(New York State Library)*

qualified voters of such state shall have participa=
ted, shall, in the absence of strong countervailing
testimony, be deemed conclusive evidence that
such state and the people thereof, are not then
in rebellion against the United States.

That attention is hereby called to an act of Con=
gress entitled "An Act to make an additional
Article of War" approved March 13. 1862, and
which Act is in the words and figures following:

Be it enacted by the Senate and House of Representatives of the United
States of America in Congress assembled, That hereafter the following
shall be promulgated as an additional article of war for the government
of the army of the United States, and shall be obeyed and observed as
such:

Article —. All officers or persons in the military or naval service of
the United States are prohibited from employing any of the forces under
their respective commands for the purpose of returning fugitives from service or labor, who may have escaped from any persons to whom such service or labor is claimed to be due, and any officer who shall be found
guilty of violating this article shall be dismissed from
the service.

Sec. 2. And be it further enacted, That this act shall take effect from
and after its passage.

Also to the ninth and tenth sections of an
Act entitled "An Act to suppress Insurrection,
to punish Treason and Rebellion, to seize and con-
fiscate property of rebels, and for other purposes,"
approved July 17. 1862, and which sections are
in the words and figures following:

Sec. 9. And be it further enacted, That all slaves of persons who
shall hereafter be engaged in rebellion against the government of the
United States, or who shall in any way give aid or comfort thereto, escaping from such persons and taking refuge within the lines of the army;
and all slaves captured from such persons or deserted by them and coming
under the control of the government of the United States; and all slaves
of such persons found on [or] being within any place occupied by rebel
forces and afterwards occupied by the forces of the United States, shall
be deemed captives of war, and shall be forever free of their servitude,
and not again held as slaves.

Sec. 10. And be it further enacted, That no slave escaping into any
State, Territory, or the District of Columbia, from any other State, shall
be delivered up, or in any way impeded or hindered of his liberty, except
for crime, or some offence against the laws, unless the person claiming said
fugitive shall first make oath that the person to whom the labor or service
of such fugitive is alleged to be due is his lawful owner, and has not borne
arms against the United States in the present rebellion, nor in any way given
aid and comfort thereto; and no person engaged in the military or naval
service of the United States shall, under any pretence whatever, assume
to decide on the validity of the claim of any person to the service or labor
of any other person, or surrender up any such person to the claimant, on
pain of being dismissed from the service.

And I do hereby enjoin upon and order all
persons engaged in the military and naval
service of the United States to observe, obey,
and enforce, within their respective spheres of
service, the act and sections above recited.

And the executive will recommend that
all citizens of the United States who shall have
remained loyal thereto throughout the rebellion, shall (upon the restoration of the constitutional relation between the United States, and
their respective states, and people, if that relation
shall have been suspended or disturbed) be
compensated for all losses by acts of the United
States, including the loss of slaves.

In witness whereof, I have
L. S. hereunto set my hand, and caused
the seal of the United States to be
affixed.

Done at the City of Washington
this twenty second day of September,
in the year of our Lord, one thousand, eight
hundred and sixty two, and, of the
Independence of the United
States the eighty seventh.

Abraham Lincoln

By the President
William H. Seward,
Secretary of State

Reaction to the Proclamation

Northerners reacted differently to the Proclamation. New York was particularly divided over the issue. Many, including Frederick Douglass and Gerrit Smith, hailed it as a moral triumph. Others objected to the idea that the war was now to be fought to free the slaves.

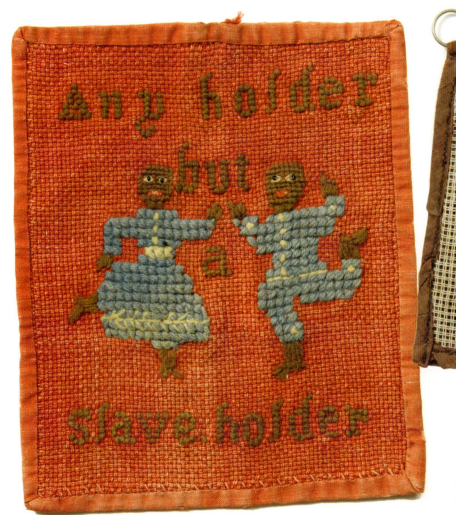

POTHOLDERS
Cross-stitched potholders celebrating President Lincoln's Emancipation Proclamation. (*Chemung County Historical Society*)

"EMANCIPATION" BY THOMAS NAST, *right*
This drawing by Thomas Nast for *Harper's Weekly* was titled, "The Emancipation of the Negroes, January 1863—And the Future." *Harper's Weekly*, January 24, 1863 (*New York State Library, Manuscripts and Special Collections*)

120

EMANCIPATION.

THE EMANCIPATION OF THE NEGROES, JANUARY, 1863—THE PAST AND THE FUTURE.—DRAWN BY MR. THOMAS NAST.—[SEE PRECEDING PAGE.]

BALLOT
New York State ballot for the election of 1862.
(New York State Museum Collection, H-2006.71.29)

OUR BEST SOCIETY, *top left*
This January 31, 1863, cartoon in *New York Illustrated News* depicts an imaginary encounter between free blacks and wealthy New Yorkers on Fifth Avenue. While many white New Yorkers opposed slavery, they were not prepared to recognize blacks as their equals.
(New York State Library, Manuscripts and Special Collections)

ENVELOPES, *left*
Civil War–era envelope printed with an image depicting a free black man and labeled "The Result of Secession."
(New York State Museum Collection, H-1977.91.7)

The Election of 1862

Politically, emancipation had significant consequences for Lincoln. The Republicans lost twenty-eight seats in Congress, though they retained a majority in both houses. From New York, nineteen of the state's thirty-one seats in the House of Representatives went Democratic. The Republican governor was replaced by Democrat Horatio Seymour. The largest state in the Union was now led by Lincoln's opposition.

Governor Horatio Seymour (1810–1886)

Born in Pompey Hill, Onondaga County, Horatio Seymour graduated from Geneva College and became an attorney in Utica. He remained committed to the preservation of the Union, but he was vocal in his opposition to emancipation, the draft, and actions—such as Lincoln's suspension of habeas corpus—that Seymour considered attacks on personal liberties.

Seymour was one of President Lincoln's most prominent Democratic opponents. Despite his opposition to the president, Seymour continued to supply men and materials to the war effort.

By 1863, New York's Democratic Party had split into competing factions. Loyal Democrats, such as Seymour, supported the Union war effort while others sympathized with the South and criticized emancipation. These divisions help fuel working-class Democratic resentments—most notably during the draft riots of 1863.

Seymour ended his career after running unsuccessfully for president against General Ulysses S. Grant in 1868.

GOVERNOR HORATIO SEYMOUR
(New York State Library, Manuscripts and Special Collections)

ERASTUS CORNING
(New York State Library, Manuscripts and Special Collections)

Erastus Corning (1794–1872)

Erastus Corning was one of nineteenth-century New York's more prosperous and influential business leaders. He grew rich in the iron industry and later in American and Canadian railroads.

Corning served as Albany's Mayor, New York State Senator, and U.S. Congressman. He was a Democrat who supported the war effort while opposing many Lincoln administration policies—particularly the administration's assertion of military over civil law.

Corning both aided and profited from the U.S. war effort. His iron works contracted with the government to produce parts for the U.S.S. *Monitor,* and his railroads carried goods and men to and from the front.

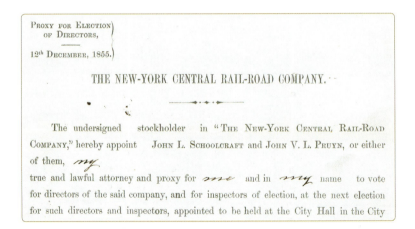

NEW YORK CENTRAL PROXY CERTIFICATE
Corning was the driving force behind the incorporation of the New York Central Railroad in 1853. He served as its president until 1864. During the war, the New York Central and other New York railroads sent men and materials to Union Armies in various theaters.
(New York State Museum Collection, H-1974.46.18)

"Departing for the Seat of the War"
This E. L. Henry work shows a New York Regiment boarding a train for Washington.
(New York State Museum Collection, H-1940.17.282)

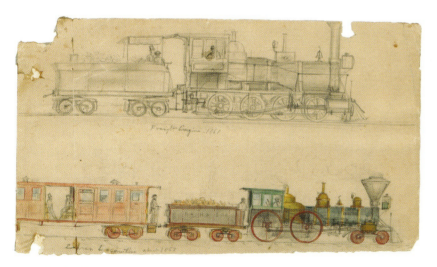

E. L. Henry Sketch
This E. L. Henry study depicts locomotives from 1858 and 1861. Railroads enabled the North to wage war on a continental scale.
(New York State Museum Collection, H-1940.17.167)

Erastus Corning and Habeas Corpus

The Lincoln administration took measures to quell dissent in areas of the North beginning in 1861 when Rebel sympathizers rioted in Maryland. The infringements on constitutional guarantees to free speech, habeas corpus, and the right to a fair trial prompted an outcry from Americans of all political persuasions.

Among the most vocal was a group of Albany Democrats led by Erastus Corning. At a meeting on May 23, 1863, the group passed a series of resolutions criticizing the Lincoln administration's heavy-handed tactics. Their letter to Lincoln prompted the President's strong defense of his rapidly expanding executive powers:

> The constitution itself makes the distinction; and I can no more be persuaded that the government can constitutionally take no strong measure in time of rebellion, because it can be shown that the same could not be lawfully taken in time of peace, than I can be persuaded that a particular drug is not good medicine for a sick man, because it can be shown to not be good food for a well one.
> *(Abraham Lincoln to Erastus Corning, June 12, 1863)*

> We have carefully considered the grounds on which your pretensions to more than regal authority are claimed to rest; and if we do not misinterpret the misty and clouded forms of expression in which those pretensions are set forth, your meaning is that while the rights of the citizen are protected by the Constitution in time of peace, they are suspended or lost in time of war, or when invasion or rebellion exist.
> *(Erastus Corning et al. to President Lincoln, June 30, 1863)*

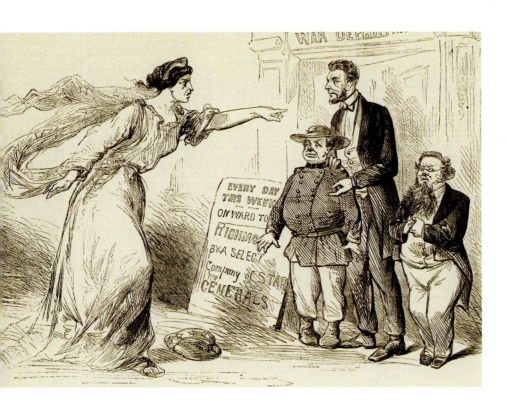

CARTOON, COLUMBIA CONFRONTING LINCOLN
The horrific casualties at the Battle of Fredericksburg threatened to turn Northern public opinion against the war effort.
Harper's Weekly, January 3, 1863
(New York State Library, Manuscripts and Special Collections)

Battle of Fredericksburg, December 13, 1862

The Battle of Fredericksburg was a major Union defeat. In November, Lincoln replaced General McClellan as commander of the Army of the Potomac with General Ambrose Burnside. Burnside was as reckless as McClellan was cautious, and he foolishly attacked Confederate troops dug in on high ground along the Rappahannock River.

Burnside ordered bridges constructed across the river and ordered frontal assaults that resulted in 12,600 Federal casualties.

New Yorkers comprised nearly 25 percent of the Army of the Potomac during the battle, including eighty of 276 infantry regiments, and were involved in some of the battle's fiercest fighting.

The disastrous military defeat at Fredericksburg caused many in the north to wonder whether President Lincoln would follow through with his threatened Emancipation Proclamation on January 1.

"The position of the enemy is most advantageous. . . . [T]he conflict will be terrible and almost every hamlet of the Free North will be filled with lamentations for some dear loved one slain. Elmira will have her share of mourning."

—Sergeant Arthur T. Williams, Company H, 50th New York Engineers

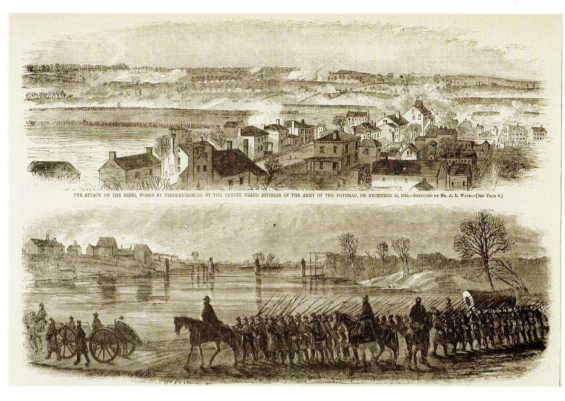

THE ATTACK ON THE REBEL WORKS AT FREDERICKSBURG BY THE CENTRE GRAND DIVISION OF THE ARMY OF THE POTOMAC, ON DECEMBER 13, 1862.—Sketched by Mr. A. R. Waud.—[See Page 6.]

THE ATTACK ON THE REBEL WORKS AT FREDERICKSBURG BY THE CENTRE GRAND DIVISION
This view of the battle from across the Rappahannock shows the heights that the Union Army had to assault.
Harper's Weekly January 3, 1863
(New York State Library, Manuscripts and Special Collections)

THE BOMBARDMENT OF FREDERICKSBURG BY THE ARMY OF THE POTOMAC
As the engineers constructed the pontoon bridges across the river, Union artillery attempted to keep Confederate sharpshooters at bay.
(New York State Library, Manuscripts and Special Collections)

50th Engineer Regiment, New York Volunteers

This regiment was organized at Elmira, Chemung County, and comprised of men from Albany to Buffalo. Under continuous fire from Confederate sharpshooters, the 50th New York Engineers suffered fifty casualties while helping to construct the pontoon bridges across the Rappahannock River.

CONSTRUCTION OF PONTOON BRIDGES ACROSS THE RAPPAHANNOCK
Men from New York's 50th Engineers were among the units tasked with constructing bridges across the Rappahannock River.
Leslie's Illustrated, February 1, 1862
(New York State Library, Manuscripts and Special Collections)

69th Infantry Regiment, New York Volunteers

To attack Marye's Heights, Union troops had to cross a canal ditch and four hundred yards of open ground. The entire charge was made against artillery and rifle fire. The Irishmen of the 69th New York made the near-suicidal attack and came within yards of Rebels behind a stone wall before being forced to take cover. Robert E. Lee reportedly praised the regiment as "The Fighting Irish."

MILITARY ACCOUTREMENTS
This cartridge box, powder flask, and belt buckle belonged to DeWitt Clinton Erwin, a soldier in the 50th Engineer Regiment, New York Volunteers. Erwin, from Painted Post, Steuben County, was one of ten children born to New York State Militia General Francis Erwin. He enlisted at age nineteen in Company F, 50th Engineers. After the war, he returned to the family farm. Erwin died in 1873 at the age of thirty.
(New York State Museum Collection, H-1928.3.2 A-B, H-1928.3.16, H-1928.3.16 D, and H-1928.3.22)

THE ATTACK ON FREDERICKSBURG—THE FORLORN HOPE SCALING THE HILL
Harper's Weekly artists attempted to capture the severity of the fighting during the Union assault on Marye's Heights.
(New York State Library, Manuscripts and Special Collections)

The Emancipation Proclamation, January 1, 1863

The Emancipation Proclamation brought both horror and jubilation to the war-torn nation. Frederick Douglass immediately called it a "freedom" document even though it did not abolish slavery everywhere or begin to address the issue of black citizenship. The proclamation did bring freedom to hundreds of thousands of enslaved people, but given the depth of racism in both the North and the South, President Lincoln knew that few white Americans were ready to accept black equality. One of the proclamation's most radical provisions called for the enrollment of black troops into military service. More than two hundred thousand black soldiers helped the Union win the war. These men also shaped the war's outcome, since military service forced the question of black citizenship onto the national agenda after the war.

PRESENTATION OF COLORS TO A COLORED REGIMENT
The 20th Regiment, United States Colored Troops, receives its Regimental Colors at Union Square.
(New York State Library, Manuscripts and Special Collections)

U.S. Issued Hat Insignia, Belt Buckle, and Cartridge Box
Governor Horatio Seymour refused to authorize the creation of African American regiments in the state. Federally created U.S. Colored Troop regiments were instead raised in New York.
(New York State Museum Collection, H-1942.34.1 and H-1957.1.5 A, H-2011.22.111)

Muster Roll Abstract for a soldier in 26th U.S. Colored Troops, *above*
(New York State Archives)

Certificate of Appointment, *left*
This document appointed Andress B. Hull as a captain in the 30th U.S. Colored Troops. African American regiments were commanded by white officers.
(New York State Library, Manuscripts and Special Collections)

Frederick Douglass

(New York State Library, Manuscripts and Special Collections)

MEN OF COLOR, TO ARMS!

A Call by Frederick Douglass.

When first the Rebel cannon shattered the walls of Sumter, and drove away its starving garrison, I predicted that the war then and there inaugurated would not be fought out entirely by white men. Every month's experience during these two dreary years has confirmed that opinion. A war undertaken and brazenly carried on for the perpetual enslavement of colored men, calls logically and loudly upon colored men to help to suppress it. Only a moderate share of sagacity was needed to see that the arm of the slave was the best defence against the arm of the slaveholder. Hence with every reverse to the National arms, with every exulting shout of victory raised by the slaveholding Rebels, I have implored the imperilled nation to unchain against her foes her powerful black hand. Slowly and reluctantly that appeal is beginning to be heeded. Stop not now to complain that it was not heeded sooner. It may, or it may not have been best—that it should not. This is not the time to discuss that question. Leave it to the future. When the war is over, the country is saved, peace is established, and the black man's rights are secured, as they will be, history with an impartial hand, will dispose of that and sundry other questions. Action! action! not criticism, is the plain duty of this hour. Words are now useful only as they stimulate to blows. The office of speech now is only to point out when, where and how to strike to the best advantage. There is no time for delay. The tide is at flood that leads on to fortune. From east to west, from north to south the sky is written all over with "now or never." Liberty won by white men would lack half its lustre. Who would be free themselves must strike the blow. Better even to die free than to live slaves. This is the sentiment of every brave colored man among us. There are weak and cowardly men in all nations. We have them among us. They will tell you that this is the "whiteman's war;" that you will be "better off after than before the war;" that the getting of you into the army is to "sacrifice you on the first opportunity." Believe them not—cowards themselves, they do not wish to have their cowardice shamed by your brave example. Leave them to their timidity, or to whatever other motive may hold them back.

I have not thought lightly of the words I am now addressing to you. The counsel I give comes of close observation of the great struggle now in progress—and of the deep conviction that this is your hour and mine.

In good earnest, then, and after the best deliberation, I, now, for the first time during the war, feel at liberty to call and counsel you to arms. By every consideration which binds you to your enslaved fellow countrymen, and the peace and welfare of your country; by every aspiration which you cherish for the freedom and equality of yourselves and your children; by all the ties of blood and identity which make us one with the brave black men now fighting our battles in Louisiana, in South Carolina, I urge you to fly to arms, and smite with death the power that would bury the Government and your liberty in the same hopeless grave. I wish I could tell you that the State of New York calls you to this high honor. For the moment her constituted authorities are silent on the subject. They will speak by and by, and doubtless on the right side; but we are not compelled to wait for her. We can get at the throat of treason and Slavery through the State of Massachusetts.

She was first in the war of Independence; first to break the chains of her slaves; first to make the black man equal before the law; first to admit colored children to her common schools, and she was the first to answer with her blood the alarm cry of the nation—when its capital was menaced by rebels. You know her patriotic Governor, and you know Charles Sumner—I need add no more.

Massachusetts now welcomes you to arms as her soldiers. She has but a small colored population from which to recruit. She has full leave of the General Government to send one regiment to the war, and she has undertaken to do it. Go quickly and help fill up this first colored regiment from the North. I am authorized to assure you that you will receive the same wages, the same rations, the same equipments, the same protection, the same treatment and the same bounty secured to white soldiers. You will be led by able and skillful officers—men who will take especial pride in your efficiency and success. They will be quick to accord to you all the honor you shall merit by your valor—and see that your rights and feelings are respected by other soldiers I have assured myself on these points—and can speak with authority. More than twenty years unswerving devotion to our common cause, may give me some humble claim to be trusted at this momentous crisis.

I will not argue. To do so implies hesitation and doubt, and you do not hesitate. You do not doubt. The day dawns—the morning star is bright upon the horizon! The iron gate of our prison stands half open. One gallant rush from the North will fling it wide open, while four millions of our brothers and sisters shall march out into Liberty! The chance is now given you to end in a day the bondage of centuries, and to rise in one bound from social degradation to the plane of common equality with all other varieties of men. Remember Denmark Vesey of Charleston. Remember Nathaniel Turner of South Hampton; remember Shields, Green, and Copeland, who followed noble John Brown, and fell as glorious martyrs for the cause of the slaves. Remember that in a contest with oppression, the Almighty has no attribute which can take sides with oppressors. The case is before you. This is our golden opportunity—let us accept it—and forever wipe out the dark reproaches unsparingly hurled against us by our enemies. Win for ourselves the gratitude of our country—and the best blessings of our posterity through all time. The nucleus of this first regiment is now in camp at Readville, a short distance from Boston. I will undertake to forward to Boston all persons adjudged fit to be mustered into this regiment, who shall apply to me at any time within the next two weeks.

FREDERICK DOUGLASS.

Rochester, March 2, 1863.

Handbill
A printed advertisement for Frederick Douglass's speech.
(New York State Office of Parks, Recreation and Historic Preservation)

United States Colored Troops

The Emancipation Proclamation authorized the recruitment of African American soldiers. Lincoln and his supporters believed that these new recruits would shift the outcome of the war in the North's favor. With a few notable exceptions, most African Americans joined federal units rather than state volunteer forces. Three regiments of United States Colored Troops were raised in New York. Eventually, 180,000 African Americans fought for the Union.

Men of Color—To Arms!

Frederick Douglass and other leading abolitionists made impassioned appeals urging African Americans to volunteer in the fight for freedom, but recruitment was slow in many Northern states. With no other place to enlist, many black New Yorkers enlisted in the Massachusetts 54th Infantry; others joined the United States Colored Troops.

NEGRO RECRUITS AS SEEN PASSING UP BEEKMAN STREET
Rikers Island and Hart Island served as training grounds for the more than four thousand blacks who joined the 20th, 26th, and 31st Regiments of United States Colored Troops being raised in New York.
New York Illustrated News, July 4, 1863 *(New York State Library, Manuscripts and Special Collections)*

PRINT, BATTLE OF GETTYSBURG

This print depicts the desperate struggle along the stone wall at the top of Cemetery Ridge on July 3, 1863, at Gettysburg. Of the 315 Northern units at Gettysburg, ninety were from New York, and New Yorkers commanded twenty-one of seventy-two brigades. Many were heavily engaged in the fighting, and New Yorkers suffered 6,800 of the Union's 23,000 casualties. *(New York State Museum Collection, H-INV 5780)*

Battle of Gettysburg, July 1–July 3, 1863

Gettysburg—the largest battle ever fought in North America—was a decisive U.S. victory. Often described as the war's turning point, it halted Lee's second invasion of the North and ended Confederate hopes of European intervention. Lee's army engaged Union Cavalry near Gettysburg, Pennsylvania, on July 1, 1863, and both sides rushed reinforcements to the area. The U.S. suffered heavy casualties during that first day but was able to retreat to strong defensive positions from which they could not be dislodged over the next two days. Forced to retreat, Lee was never again able to invade the North.

PRINT, "THE REPULSE OF LONGSTREET'S ASSAULT."
This print of the battle's second day portrays the struggle near Little Round Top at Gettysburg. Several New York regiments were heavily involved in the fighting.
(New York State Museum Collection, H-INV 2440)

A Terrible Fascination
Civil War Photography

The development of photography meant, for the first time, that the horrors of the battlefield could be seen on the home front. When New York photographer Mathew Brady exhibited "The Dead at Antietam" in October 1862 in his New York City gallery, the public was immediately confronted by the carnage of war. Photographers frequently traveled with Northern armies, sending pictures back to audiences at home. No longer were the dead confined to lists of names published in local newspapers.

Sergeant Andrew Guthrie, Mumford, Monroe County (1840–1930)

The son of Scottish and Irish immigrants, Andrew Guthrie was born in Caledonia, Livingston County, April 26, 1840. As a child, Guthrie worked on the family farm in nearby Mumford.

In 1861, along with other young men from Mumford, he enlisted in the Company K, 8th New York Volunteer Cavalry at Rochester. Private Guthrie was promoted to sergeant in 1863. The 8th New York Cavalry was part of General John Buford's Division that encountered Confederate forces near Gettysburg, Pennsylvania, on July 1, 1863.

His service record indicates his capture, imprisonment in Libby Prison in Richmond, and subsequent exchange for Confederate prisoners.

8TH NEW YORK GROUP PHOTOGRAPH
Private Andrew Guthrie (seated second from right) and fellow soldiers following their enlistment with the 8th New York Volunteer Cavalry. Guthrie's close friend James Blair (standing left) was captured at the Battle of Malvern Hill, Virginia. Three months before the end of the war James Blair died in Andersonville Prison in Georgia. *(Courtesy of Jean Guthrie)*

ANDREW GUTHRIE'S BINOCULARS, PISTOL, SABER, AND CAP POUCH
These accoutrements belonged to Private Guthrie. His was one of the units that first confronted the Confederates at Gettysburg early on July 1, 1863. During the war, the 8th New York Cavalry would see action in more than fifty battles. Guthrie received a saber wound to the face and bore the scar all of his life. *(Courtesy of Jean Guthrie)*

THE FEDERAL DEAD AT GETTYSBURG, *far left*
This photograph of Union troops killed on the first day at Gettysburg was taken by Timothy O'Sullivan. *(Library of Congress)*

Generals Daniel Sickles and Gouverneur K. Warren

Several New York generals played critical roles during the Battle of Gettysburg, including Daniel Sickles and Gouverneur K. Warren. Major General Sickles remains a controversial figure for his actions at Gettysburg on the second day of the battle. Sickles, the commander of the U.S. III Corps, disobeyed orders and moved his troops a mile forward from their defensive positions along Cemetery Ridge. This left the III Corps exposed at both flanks, and the unit suffered heavy losses.

Warren recognized that the Union's critically important defensive position at Little Round Top—abandoned by Sickles's Corps—was undefended. He dispatched the nearest available troops to the scene. They arrived just in time to repel a Confederate assault that involved some of the most intense fighting of the war. Warren's actions secured the Union flank and forced General Lee into a final desperate attempt to break the Union lines on July 3.

DANIEL SICKLES

Sickles, a Democratic politician from New York City, was a classic "political general" who used his influence to obtain his commission. He had no military experience, but Lincoln—seeking favor with New York Democrats—authorized Sickles to form the Excelsior Brigade. Sickles was a colorful figure and an infamous ladies man in antebellum New York. As a Congressman, he had once killed his wife's lover, only to be acquitted on a temporary insanity plea.

Some critics have since argued that Sickles put the entire Union defense at risk, while others have claimed that his maneuver inadvertently blunted the Confederate offensive. During the fighting at Gettysburg, Sickles was struck in the leg by a cannon ball. The leg was amputated, ending his military career. After the war, Sickles was a driving force for the erection of monuments at the battlefield. *(New York State Library, Manuscripts and Special Collections)*

GOUVERNEUR K. WARREN
General Gouverneur K. Warren, of Cold Springs, Putnam County, is widely remembered as the "Hero of Little Round Top."
(New York State Library, Manuscripts and Special Collections)

GENERAL WARREN'S PRESENTATION SWORD
This sword was given to General Gouverneur K. Warren by the citizens of Cold Springs in recognition of his actions during the Battle of Gettysburg.
(New York State Museum Collection, H-1936.9.2 A-G)

The Enrollment Act of 1863 . . .
Rich Man's War, Poor Man's Fight

As the war dragged on and the need for new soldiers increased, Congress authorized a military draft with the passage of the Enrollment Act in March 1863. This legislation exacerbated pre-war tensions between blacks and whites, and native-born and immigrant populations. It also enabled men with money to avoid being drafted. This caused intense controversy, particularly among working-class immigrants in cities such as New York and Troy.

The Enrollment Act required all eligible men between the ages of eighteen and forty-five to register for the draft. Federal administrators established quotas, and as the most populous state, New York was required to furnish more men than any other state.

DRAFT NOTICES
These notices were issued to those men whose names were called for the draft.
(New York State Library, Manuscripts and Special Collections)

DUPLICATE.

No. 43

Office of Receiver of Commutation Money,

22d District of *New York*

Received at *Oswego* on the 15th day of *August* 1863 from *Artemus Benedict* who was drafted into the service of the United States on the 5th day of *August* 1863, from the 22d Congressional District of the State of *New York* the sum of *Three Hundred (300)* Dollars, to obtain, under Section 13 of the "Act for enrolling and calling out the National forces, and for other purposes," approved March 3d, 1863, discharge from further liability under that draft.

Ralph H. Avery
Receiver of Commutation Money.

U. S. SUBSTITUTE & VOLUNTEER AGENCY.

Capt. E. COMBS,

(Formerly Captain of Company B 5th Regiment Heavy Artillery, N. Y. Vols.)

Office, No. 50 LISPENARD STREET, NEAR BROADWAY,

NEW YORK,

RESPECTFULLY OFFERS HIS SERVICES TO

MERCHANTS, BANKERS, MANUFACTURERS,

AND OTHERS.

SUBSTITUTES FURNISHED,

AND

EXEMPTION CERTIFICATES FOR 3 YEARS, OBTAINED FOR PERSONS ENROLLED AND LIABLE TO A DRAFT,

AND ALSO FOR

DRAFTED GENTLEMEN.

COMMUTATION RECEIPT
This draft notice for Artemus Benedict of Oswego County is accompanied by a receipt indicating that he paid $300 to exempt himself from the draft.
(New York State Library, Manuscripts and Special Collections)

HANDBILL, U.S. SUBSTITUTE & VOLUNTEER AGENCY
Men with enough money could avoid the draft by paying substitutes to take their place. This increased the perception that the war was being disproportionately fought by the poor while the wealthy prospered.
(New York State Museum Collection, H-1983.1.2)

141

Troubles in the Metropolis
The New York City Draft Riots

Many consider the New York City Draft Riots the worst civil disturbance in American history. On July 13, 1863, shortly after the first draft numbers were drawn, mobs of working-class Irish and others destroyed or ransacked public and private buildings. They attacked policemen, and beat, tortured, and lynched more than one hundred African Americans. The mobs blamed blacks for the war. Thousands of troops were called back from Pennsylvania—where many of them had recently fought in the Battle of Gettysburg—and they restored order by July 16. The riots caused more than one million dollars in property damage and ruined countless lives.

"This mob is testing the Government nearly as strongly as the Southern rebellion. If you cannot enforce the draft here, it will not be enforced elsewhere."
—*Edward S. Sanford, U.S. Military Telegraph Service, New York City, to Secretary of War Edwin Stanton, July 14, 1863*

CHARGE OF THE POLICE ON THE RIOTERS AT THE TRIBUNE OFFICE
When violent riots against the draft erupted in July, local police in New York City were overwhelmed by the mobs. Troops were rushed from Pennsylvania to suppress the uprising. *Harper's Weekly*, August 1, 1863
(*New York State Museum Collection, H-1973.211.56*)

THE MEETING OF FRIENDS
Horatio Seymour attempted to calm the mob by addressing them directly. He restated his belief that the draft was unconstitutional but argued against violence. Seymour's referral to the mob as "My Friends," however, sparked condemnation by his political opponents and contributed to his electoral defeat in 1864.
(*New York State Library, Manuscripts and Special Collections*)

THE RIOTS AT NEW YORK—THE RIOTERS BURNING AND SACKING THE COLORED ORPHAN ASYLUM.—[See Page 494.]

SACKING THE COLORED ORPHAN ASYLUM
The New York City Draft Riots were an attack on the entire black community,
not just black men. Mobs also targeted African American women and children.
Harper's Weekly, August 1, 1863 *(New York State Library, Manuscripts and Special Collections)*

Gibbs Carbine

This Gibbs carbine was awaiting shipment to the army when the Draft Riots broke out. New York police reportedly commandeered these weapons before crowds attacked the Armory at Second Avenue and 21st Street. *(New York State Museum Collection, H-1971.64.2)*

Knapsack

When Robert E. Lee invaded Pennsylvania, Governor Seymour dispatched the New York Militia to assist in the defense of Harrisburg. This left New York City with no militia reserve. The troops that were rushed from Pennsylvania to quell the riots included the 7th Regiment, New York State Militia. *(New York State Museum Collection, H-1947.4.9)*

Draft Cards

Draft cards from a precinct in New York City detailing name, occupation, and district. Every man eligible for the draft was required to fill out a similar card. *(New-York Historical Society)*

WHITE SLAVES.

It is of the greatest importance to the workingmen of the United States to understand the true sentiments and objects of the leading traitors of the South. Their opinions of workingmen---who earn their support by their daily labor--- are clearly set forth in the following extract from the speech of Mr. Hammond, of South Carolina, in the Senate of the United States, on the 4th of March, 1858.

"In all social systems there must be a class to do the mean duties, to perform the drudgery of life---that is, a class requiring but a low order of intellect, and but little skill. Its requisites are vigor, docility, fidelity. . . . . It constitutes the very mud-sills of society and of political government; and you might as well attempt to build a house in the air, as to build either one or the other except on the mud-sills. Fortunately for the South, she found a race adapted to that purpose to her hand. . . . We use them for the purpose, and call them slaves. The man who lives by daily labor, and scarcely lives at that, and who has to put out his labor in the market, and take the best he can get for it---in short, your whole class of manual laborers and operatives, as you call them, are SLAVES. The difference between us is, that our slaves are hired for life, and well compensated; there is no starvation, no begging, no want of employment among our people, and not too much employment either. Yours are hired by the day. . . . YOUR SLAVES ARE WHITE, OF YOUR OWN RACE---you are brothers, of one blood. Our slaves do not vote. We give them no political power. Yours do vote; and, being the majority, they are the depositories of all your political power. If they knew the tremendous secret, that the ballot-box is stronger than an army with bayonets, where would you be!---Your society would be reconstructed. . . . Not by meetings in parks, with arms in their hands, but by the peaceful process of the ballot-box."

The law-abiding and union-loving workingmen of the Union---whom the Senator denounces as "White Slaves," went to the ballot-box, according to the Constitution, and effected "a peaceful revolution." But the "gentlemen" traitors of the South, less loyal and less honest, went "with arms in their hands," and treason in their hearts, and have compelled the workingmen of the South to rise against their brothers of the North, in order to make "white slaves" of them all.

There are many other advocates of the doctrine of Senator Hammond who can be produced.

These things being true, I charge,

1st. That the rebellion of the South Carolina traitors is an attempt to destroy the interests of the democratic working classes of the Union.

2d. That it is an effort to build up forever a system by which "*Capital shall own Labor.*"

3d. That it is an attempt to make slavery---and property in slaves---the controlling interest of the Union.

4th. That Slavery is, and from its nature must be, the deadly enemy of Free Labor.

5th. That the success of the traitors will be a death-blow to the interests of Free Workingmen, North and South.

6th. That self-interest and patriotism both call upon Workingmen to stand by the government firm as a rock till the rebellion is put down, and peace restored by the constitutional authorities.

I challenge Hon. Fernando Wood, Hon. Benjamin Wood, C. Godfrey Gunther, Esq. and Prof. Mason, of New York; F. W. Hughes, Esq. and Hon. Geo. B. Woodward, of Pennsylvania; and Hon. C. L. Vallandigham and Hon. G. E. Pugh, of Ohio, to disprove my quotations or the correctness of my conclusions.

A Democratic Workingman.

NEW YORK, Sept. 28th, 1863.   ☞ PLEASE POST THIS UP.
Sold by SINCLAIR TOUSEY, 121 Nassau Street, New York.

Broadside

Many working-class whites resented being forced to fight a war for emancipation, which they believed would create a source of cheap labor in direct competition to their interests. *(New York State Library, Manuscripts and Special Collections)*

From the earliest days of the war, Northern civilians sought ways to contribute to the war effort. The United States Sanitary Commission (U.S.S.C.), a philanthropic humanitarian organization whose goal was to bring modern medical relief to soldiers on the battlefield, was established in 1861. Through an adjunct agency, the Women's Central Relief Association, the commission established a national network to distribute the many products of soldiers' aid societies, such as bandages, clothing, and food.

Aid for the Troops

Relief Societies, Bazaars, and Sanitary Fairs

Women in New York played a pivotal role in supporting the war effort. From the start, they assumed leadership roles in local civic organizations aimed at providing relief to soldiers. As the fighting continued, the scope of their endeavors expanded. The Women's Central Relief Association of New York had been a driving force behind the creation of the U.S.S.C. The U.S.S.C. was a private agency charged with supporting sick and wounded U.S. soldiers. Frederick Law Olmsted directed the Commission, which operated in the Northern states. It was supported by volunteers and private funds—often raised through fairs featuring exhibitions, auctions, and art displays. New Yorkers raised significant sums through fairs across the state:

December 1863—Rochester ($10,319)

February 1864—Brooklyn and Long Island ($403,000)

February 1864—Albany ($83,000)

April 1864—New York Metropolitan ($2,000,000)

MAKING HAVELOCKS FOR THE VOLUNTEERS
In New York City, the Metropolitan Fair raised nearly $2,000,000 to benefit the troops. *Harper's Weekly*, June 29, 1861
(*New York State Library, Manuscripts and Special Collections*)

TICKET
Ticket to a Sanitary Fair in
Elmira, Chemung County
(Chemung County Historical Society)

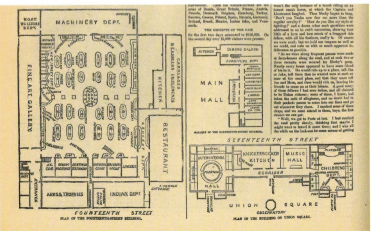

THE ARMY RELIEF BAZAAR
In February 1864, Albany's civic organizations organized a massive
bazaar in Washington Park to raise money for soldiers' aid.
(New York State Museum Collection, H-1982.76.15)

MAP OF METROPOLITAN FAIR
The Metropolitan Fair in Manhattan was a gigantic affair with many
of the venues encompassing entire city blocks.
Harper's Weekly, April 16, 1864
(New York State Library, Manuscripts and Special Collections)

ARMY RELIEF BAZAAR BUILDINGS—ACADEMY PARK,
ALBANY, February, 1864.

ORIGINAL DRAFT
OF THE
President's First Emancipation Proclamation,

DATED SEPTEMBER 22, 1862.

Ticket No. 243   Issued to _C. M. Throop, Schorie, N.Y._

The holder of this Ticket has contributed ONE DOLLAR to the Bazaar in aid of
the Sanitary Commission for the Benefit of our Sick and Wounded Soldiers.

William Barnes, Chairman.

JOHN K. PORTER,   EDWARD C. DELAVAN, } Special
GERRIT SMITH,   THOMAS W. OLCOTT,   } Committee.
JAMES A. BELL,   WILLIAM C. BRYANT, }

RAFFLE TICKET
Secretary of State Seward arranged for a draft copy of the Preliminary Emancipation Proclamation to be sent to Albany in time for its Relief Bazaar. The document, written in President Lincoln's own hand, was won by abolitionist Gerrit Smith. It was later purchased by the New York State Legislature and donated to the State Library. (_New York State Library, Manuscripts and Special Collections_)

NEEDLEWORK CASE
This tartan-covered needlework case is inscribed, "Bought at the Army Relief Bazaar Feb. 25, 1864." Because the case is covered in a lacquered paper printed with a "Stuart tartan" pattern, it may have been purchased at the Bazaar's Scotch Booth, though sewing implements such as this were popular at many booths at the Bazaar. (_Albany Institute of History & Art_)

SCOTCH BOOTH
This photograph depicts several members of the Army Relief Bazaar's Scotch Booth. All are fully attired in traditional Scottish clothing. (_New York State Library, Manuscripts and Special Collections_)

DOLLS

These dolls were purchased at the Albany Army Relief Bazaar by Mr. and Mrs. Thurlow Weed as a gift for Kitty Van Antwerp. They descended to her daughter Martha Van Antwerp Stanton Easton, and her granddaughter Phoebe Powell Bender, the donor. The female doll's wardrobe is comprised of fifty-eight sets of outerwear, underwear, and matching accessories (hats, shoes, parasols, etc.). The clothes, made by Kitty's aunt Amelia King (died 1867) who married John McMurray, are miniature reproductions of Mrs. McMurray's trousseau. *(Albany Institute of History & Art)*

"There was an old Woman — she lived in a Shoe
She had so many children; she didn't know what to do"!

Mrs Kitty Van Antwerp

(rest unknown).

KITTY VAN ANTWERP
Photograph of Kitty Van Antwerp, daughter of Mr. and Mrs. John E. Van Antwerp of Albany. Wearing a shawl, lappets, lace cap, and child-sized spectacles atop her head, Kitty, every bit the Lilliputian Dutch matriarch, is perched in her paper shoe prop surrounded by an extended family of seventeen dolls. *(Albany Institute of History & Art)*

EMILY WEED BARNES
Signature card with a photograph of Emily Weed Barnes.
(New York State Library, Manuscripts and Special Collections)

Emily Barnes (1827–1889)

Daughter of newspaper mogul and Republican boss Thurlow Weed, Emily Weed Barnes was married to prominent Albany Republican William Barnes. On November 2, 1861, Barnes was named Recording Secretary for the Albany Army Relief Association.

An active member of Albany's civic life, Emily Weed Barnes worked tirelessly to rally support for the Union war effort. As secretary, Barnes played a leading role in organizing the Army Relief Bazaar and in securing the fair's most prized possession— a draft copy of President Lincoln's Emancipation Proclamation.

Harriet Newell Walton Wing (1815–1887)

In Queensbury, Warren County, local efforts to support soldiers through contributions of clothing, foodstuffs, and letters of support were organized and led by Harriet Wing, Secretary of the Warren County Women's Sanitary Commission chapter.

Mrs. Wing was also a founding member of the Ladies' Patriotic Association in Glens Falls, a fundraising group of women in the community.

In 1863–64, Mrs. Wing reported raising more than $700 and that more than $200 worth of flannel was received to make garments. Eleven boxes of foodstuffs had been sent for distribution along with hospital stores, cash, and materials.

"Come to the Soldier's Aid"
Mother and wife and maid.
There's a soldier away at the South
Whose lips have been pressed to your mouth,

With mutual kisses and mutual vows,
As father or son, as brother or spouse,
Who, lying now in his blood and dirt
Would weep with joy for a fresh clean shirt,
O, say, shall that brave one fret and grieve
When here is one, only wanting a sleeve,
At the rooms of the Soldier's Aid.

(Poem published in January 1863 meeting announcement for the Ladies' Patriotic Association, Queensbury)

United States Sanitary Commission

Shortly after the start of the Civil War, more than four thousand women met at Cooper Union in New York City to discuss ways women could support the war effort. The meeting resulted in the creation of the Women's Central Association of Relief. This association pressed the Lincoln administration to focus on the sanitary needs of the soldiers, prompting the creation of the United States Sanitary Commission (U.S.S.C.). While the U.S.S.C. was led predominantly by men, the majority of its accomplishments were the result of thousands of women volunteers across the North.

OFFICERS AND NURSES OF THE UNITED STATES SANITARY COMMISSION
The need for medical personnel opened many opportunities for women, most notably as nurses, and thousands of women volunteered to care for sick and wounded soldiers.
(Library of Congress)

WOMEN OF THE WOMEN'S CENTRAL ASSOCIATION OF RELIEF
Louisa Lee Schuyler (seated third from the left) and her colleagues at the Cooper Union offices of the Women's Central Association of Relief. Louisa Lee Schuyler of New York City was granddaughter of General Philip Schuyler and Alexander Hamilton. Schuyler also became chairman of the Committee on Correspondence and Publicity of the U.S.S.C., and wrote letters and reports, and lectured about the Commission's efforts. *(Courtesy of Sara Harmon)*

In 1861, President Lincoln authorized the formation of the U.S.S.C. to raise private funds to aid in the care and treatment of Union soldiers. The commission organized fundraising and published informational manuals for troops on hygiene and camp life to reduce the spread of disease. Money raised by New York's sanitary fairs was distributed by the Sanitary Commission for the purchase of medical supplies to the troops.

Louisa Lee Schuyler (1837–1926)

During the Civil War, Louisa Lee Schuyler helped organize and became secretary of the Women's Central Association of Relief. In charge of organizing all services needed by the Union soldiers, the Sanitary Commission created an independent system of transportation to ensure the receipt of supplies, prepared simple health pamphlets to train inexperienced officers about field nutrition and campsite selection, and disbursed almost $5 million in cash and more than $15 million in supplies. Under Louisa's leadership, twenty-five thousand packages were successfully classified and forwarded to Northern troops, with only one package lost.

Civil War Medicine

While the wounds and trauma of battle were horrific, disease actually killed two soldiers for every one that died on the battlefield. As new recruits poured into camps, many were exposed for the first time to diseases such as typhoid and cholera. Epidemics in the camps were common, and wounded soldiers ran risks of infection that often proved deadlier than bullets.

LOUISA LEE SCHUYLER
(New York State Library, Manuscripts and Special Collections)

Civil War Surgeon's Kit
A Civil War–era surgeon's kit similar to one that would have been used by Dr. Mary Walker. *(Onondaga Historical Association)*

Crutch
Civil War–era crutch, purchased with funds raised by the U.S.S.C.
(New York State Museum Collection, H-1971.90.10 A)

Artillery Shell with Minié balls embedded
New research suggests that between 750,000 and 800,000 soldiers died during the Civil War. Of these, approximately one-third died of wounds. Advances in military technology made these wounds increasingly difficult to treat. The Minié ball was made of soft lead that expanded upon impact, causing deadly trauma to the body. Wounds to the abdomen or chest were nearly always fatal. For wounds to the limbs, doctors had little choice but amputation.
(New York State Museum Collection, H-1961.3.8 and H-1962.1.1)

Bullets
Minié balls and bullets from the battlefield at Antietam. The increased accuracy of rifles and cannons and the deadly effect of new ammunition resulted in horrific casualties on both sides.
(New York State Military Museum, Division of Military and Naval Affairs)

Dr. Mary E. Walker (1832–1919)

Oswego native Mary Edwards Walker was the first female surgeon in the U.S. Army. A graduate of Syracuse Medical College, Walker practiced medicine in Rome, Oneida County, before the war.

When hostilities broke out, she served as a nurse and volunteer surgeon at Bull Run and other battles. She was captured in 1864 and imprisoned in Richmond for four months. Upon her release, she was commissioned as an acting assistant surgeon. After the war, Walker became a leading advocate for women's rights.

DR. MARY E. WALKER
On November 11, 1865, Dr. Mary Walker received the Medal of Honor—the only woman ever to receive the nation's highest military award. The award was rescinded in 1917, but restored in 1977 by President Jimmy Carter. *(New York State Library, Manuscripts and Special Collections)*

Walt Whitman (1819–1892)

Born on Long Island, Walt Whitman had become a renowned poet and essayist by the time the Civil War began. An opponent of slavery, Whitman, however, viewed abolitionism as a threat to the nation's democracy.

Whitman's brother George had volunteered for service in the Union Army. When George was wounded in battle, Whitman traveled to Washington to tend to him. He was so moved by the wounded soldiers that he remained in the capital. Whitman volunteered as a nurse in Army hospitals around the city. He wrote eloquently of the suffering of the sick and wounded.

". . . these thousands, and tens and twenties of thousands of American young men, badly wounded, all sorts of wounds, operated on, pallid with diarrhea, languishing, dying with fever, pneumonia, &c. open a new world somehow to me, giving closer insights, new things, exploring deeper mines than any yet, showing our humanity . . ."

—*Walt Whitman*

WALT WHITMAN
America's great poet and New York native Walt Whitman served as a nurse during the war.
(New York State Library, Manuscripts and Special Collections)

Death and Mourning in the Civil War

The Civil War claimed the lives of at least 620,000 Americans, roughly 2 percent of the total U.S. population. Nearly everyone was affected—socially, economically, and spiritually.

As casualties mounted, funerary practices became increasingly professionalized. Embalming became a widely accepted practice for the first time—this made it possible to transport men killed at the front to their loved ones at home. For many other mourners, however, bodies were never found, and there was nothing to bury.

"I regret to say that it is impossible to procure the remains of Byram. I would use every endeavor to that end if there was any possible chance of success . . . the graves are near where the men fell. There must have been nearly six hundred dead buried in the space of three hundred yards . . ."

——*Captain Samuel Simms, 51st New York Volunteers, to B. F. Howes, Esq., January 3, 1863*

PORTRAIT—GEORGE KOONS
George Koons, a teacher from Albany County, was killed near Fredericksburg, Virginia.
(New York State Museum Collection, H-1945.1.4)

157

At a meeting of the Groesbeckville Mission M. E. Sunday School. held May 10th 1863 the following preamble and Resolutions were unanimously adopted.

Whereas: Intelligence has been communicated to this School. of the death of one of our Teachers – Lieut. George H. Koons of the 43rd Regt. New-York State Volunteers, who fell while gallantly storming the Rebel Entrenchments at Fredericksburg Heights:

Resolved: That in the sudden and untimely death of Lieut. Koons. this School has lost an earnest friend and faithful Teacher – his Sorrow-Stricken Father and Mother, a dearly Cherished Son – his brothers and Sisters, a Brother bound to them by the tenderest ties – Society a useful member. and our Country, a noble defender.

Resolved: that in thus laying down his life on his Countrys Altar. Lieut. Koons has given the strongest proof of Patriotism and Loyalty to the Government of our Fathers. and of devotion to the cause of Human Liberty: And. that while we deplore the loss of our departed friend we will ever Cherish with gratitude the memory of his many virtues. and if need be, emulate his spirit of self Sacrifice in the cause for which he so heroically Suffered. and so nobly died.

Resolved:

That the Secretary be instructed to communicate to the Family of Lieut. Koons. the assurance of our heartfelt Sympathy. and sincere Condolence with them in this their sore bereavement; and that we Commend them for Consolation in this dark hour of affliction. to God. and the word of His Grace.

Samuel J Hopkins Supt   Harvey R Watson Sec'y

MANUSCRIPT
This resolution mourning the death of Lieutenant Koons cites the loss of a gifted educator and a beloved neighbor. (New York State Museum Collection, H-1945.1.2)

RETURN OF FALLEN UNION SOLDIERS TO THE NORTH
A January 21, 1865, *Leslie's Illustrated* print depicts the exhumation of Union soldiers on Southern battlefields for return to the North.
(New York State Library, Manuscripts and Special Collections)

ARRIVAL OF A BODY TO BE EMBALMED
New York City physician Thomas Holmes developed the modern chemical embalming process. Elmer Ellsworth was the first Civil War soldier to be embalmed. As the war progressed, embalming surgeons were attached to Union Army field hospitals, as depicted in *New York Illustrated News*.
(New York State Library, Manuscripts and Special Collections)

Lieutenant Colonel Elias Peissner

Born on September 5, 1825 in Vilseck, Bavaria, Elias Peissner immigrated to America in 1849 following Bavaria's failed democratic revolution. He became a professor of economics at Union College and settled in Schenectady. When war broke out, Peissner and his brother-in-law, Charles Lewis, joined the 119th New York Volunteers. Peissner rose to the rank of regimental commander and was killed leading his men during the Battle of Chancellorsville.

> "We say 'but one,' never thinking that one was somebody's all perhaps. Had a million been slain, it would have been 'only one' in a million homes."
>
> —*Charles Lewis, Fall 1863*

ARTILLERY VALISE AND CARTRIDGE BOX
These personal effects belonged to Colonel Elias Peissner.
(New York State Museum Collection, H-1971.90.1, H-1971.90.7, H-1971.91.5)

ELIAS PEISSNER
Lieutenant Colonel Elias Peissner
(Schenectady County Historical Society)

MRS. PEISSNER WITH HER BROTHER, CHARLES LEWIS
Photograph of Elias Peissner's widow Margaret and his brother-in-law. Margaret is dressed in mourning attire. With so many men gone to war, the duty of mourning often fell to women on the home front. Women were now the source of strength for the grieving family.
(Special Collections, Schaffer Library, Union College)

Civil War Prisons

When Confederate leaders refused to exchange black prisoners of war, the Union Army halted the practice of exchange. Many believed this would also starve the South of badly needed manpower. Most Civil War prisons were established in hastily made camps or by repurposing old buildings. Virtually none was designed to house the masses of men sent to them from the front. Conditions were horrid; thousands on both sides died of disease and starvation.

LIBBY PRISON
An old warehouse in Richmond's Tobacco Row, Libby Prison housed captured Union officers until 1864. Overcrowding and poor sanitation caused the death of many inmates. *Harper's Weekly*, October 17, 1863 *(New York State Library, Manuscripts and Special Collections)*

THE PRISON PEN AT MILLEN, GEORGIA, *right*
Leslie's Illustrated, January 28, 1865
(New York State Library, Manuscripts and Special Collections)

ANDERSONVILLE, LITHOGRAPH

This lithograph was produced from a sketch made by Felix La Baume, a soldier in the 39th New York Volunteers, while a prisoner at Andersonville. Arguably the most notorious Confederate prison camp, Andersonville was located in rural Sumter County, Georgia. The camp, 16½ acres surrounded by a wooden stockade, was constructed in January 1864 to hold ten thousand Union prisoners. By August, thirty-three thousand had arrived at Andersonville. In its fifteen months of operation, thirteen thousand Union soldiers died at the prison of malnutrition, exposure, and disease. *(New York State Museum Collection, H-INV 2060)*

Fort Lafayette in New York Harbor Where Political Prisoners are Confined

In 1861, President Lincoln suspended several civil liberties allowing for the detention of civilians by the Army. Constructed during the War of 1812 as part of the harbor defenses for New York City, Fort Lafayette became a prison that housed many of these Northern citizens sympathetic to the Southern cause—Copperheads. It became known as the "American Bastille." *Harper's Weekly*, September 7, 1861 *(New York State Library, Manuscripts and Special Collections)*

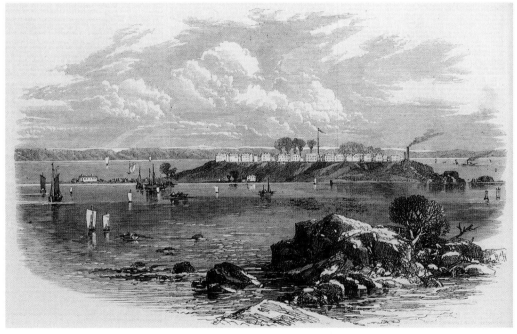

Hart's Island

An island on Long Island Sound, Hart's Island served as a prisoner of war camp for four months in early 1865. Of the 3,413 Confederate prisoners held on the island, 245 died. They were interred at Cypress Hill Cemetery in Brooklyn in 1941.
(New York State Library, Manuscripts and Special Collections)

The Elmira Prison Camp

The United States opened the Elmira Prison Camp in July 1864 to accommodate the government's increasing numbers of Rebel prisoners. The camp closed fifteen months later. Originally a barracks for five thousand men, Elmira—known as "Hellmira" by its inmates—housed more than twelve thousand Confederate soldiers. Nearly 25 percent of them died from malnutrition, exposure, and disease.

A VOLUNTEER REGIMENT ON PARADE AT THE CAMP AT ELMIRA, NEW YORK
Originally built as a mustering point known as Camp Rathbun, the camp's barracks were converted to house rebel prisoners in 1864. *Harper's Weekly*, August 17, 1861
(New York State Library, Manuscripts and Special Collections)

THIMBLE, NECKLACE, AND BRACELET
To pass the time, many prisoners made simple items such as these. Often, these trinkets were exchanged with locals for food and other badly needed supplies. *(Chemung County Historical Society)*

John Jones (1817–1900)

Born into slavery in Leesburg, Virginia, John W. Jones escaped to freedom in 1844 and established himself in Elmira. He served as an Underground Railroad conductor and is believed to have helped some eight hundred fugitive slaves escape to Canada.

During the war, Jones oversaw the burial of the 2,963 Confederate soldiers who died at Elmira. Thanks to his meticulous recordkeeping, only seven were unidentified.

CHAIR
This chair was constructed by Confederate prisoners at Elmira.
(Chemung County Historical Society)

RESTRAINING CHAIN
Restraining chain from Elmira Prison Camp.
(Chemung County Historical Society)

JOHN W. JONES
(New York State Office of Parks, Recreation and Historic Preservation)

Civil War Weddings

Doctor Tarbell and Mary Lucy Conant met one another while attending school at the Groton Academy in Groton, Tompkins County. The two became childhood sweethearts and maintained a steady correspondence during Doctor's military service.

After his capture at Winchester, Virginia, Doctor Tarbell was feared killed. Neither Tarbell's family nor Mary learned of his fate until a telegraph arrived informing them of his release from Libby Prison. Following his parole in 1865, Doctor was given thirty days leave during which he returned to Peruville to wed Mary Conant. Their honeymoon was short-lived, though. Tarbell returned to his unit, where he served the remainder of the war, mustering out as a Brevet Major on July 27, 1865.

CIVIL WAR WEDDING
This April 4, 1863, *Harper's Weekly* drawing depicts a wartime wedding. With the fear and uncertainty of going off to war, many young couples opted to be married first. The average age for a woman to be married was between eighteen and twenty-one. For men it was twenty-three. At age twenty-seven, Doctor and Mary Tarbell wed much later than was the norm for the time.
(New York State Library, Manuscripts and Special Collections)

Doctor Tarbell (1838–1895)

Born in Groton, Tompkins County, Doctor Tarbell worked on the family farm. With the outbreak of war, he enlisted in the 32nd New York Volunteer Infantry. In June 1862, he received a commission as an officer.

Tarbell fought at the battles at Antietam, Chancellorsville, and Gettysburg. He was taken prisoner in September 1864 near Winchester, Virginia, and sent to Libby Prison in Richmond. He was paroled in February 1865.

After his marriage to Mary Lucy Conant, Tarbell returned to his company. After the war, Tarbell had a successful career as a local businessman and county official. He died in 1895.

Mary Tarbell (1838–1899)

Mary Conant was born in Charlton, Massachusetts. At a very young age, she was sent to be raised by her aunt and uncle in Groton and later Peruville. Mary attended Groton Academy where she met and befriended Doctor Tarbell.

As a well-educated young woman, Mary maintained a lengthy correspondence with her sweetheart after his departure for the war in May 1861. After the war, Doctor and Mary had three children: George Schuyler, born July 15, 1868, Bertha Mary, born December 15, 1872, and Clarence D., born May 5, 1878, in Ithaca. Following Doctor's death, Mary applied for a widow's pension based on his Civil War service. Mary Tarbell died in 1899.

DOCTOR TARBELL
In September 1864, Doctor Tarbell was captured in battle near Winchester, Virginia, and sent to the infamous Libby Prison in Richmond. Given his gaunt appearance, this image of Doctor Tarbell was likely taken shortly after his release from Libby.
(Tompkins County History Center)

DOCTOR AND MARY TARBELL
A photograph of Doctor and Mary Tarbell taken at an unknown time during Doctor's military service. *(Tompkins County History Center)*

THE TARBELL FAMILY
Doctor and Mary Tarbell with their first two children, circa 1873. Tarbell left the Army in July 1865 and returned to Ithaca. He became a successful local entrepreneur and worked in the life insurance business. He was elected Tompkins County Clerk in 1870 and re-elected in 1873. *(Tompkins County History Center)*

PIN
Pin with photo of Doctor Tarbell.
(Tompkins County History Center)

Mary E. Conant.

CONANT AND TARBELL NAME CARDS
These cards are printed with Mary Tarbell's maiden name and the couple's married name. They were likely souvenirs for the wedding guests. *(Tompkins County History Center)*

HANDKERCHIEF HOLDER
Mary Tarbell's handkerchief holder. *(Tompkins County History Center)*

WEDDING DRESS BELONGING TO MARY TARBELL
This dress was worn by Mary Conant for her marriage to Doctor Tarbell, March 15, 1865. White fabric was expensive and difficult to keep clean. In the nineteenth century, it was deemed practical to marry in a colored dress. Wedding dresses were chosen so they could be worn for other formal occasions. *(Tompkins County History Center)*

171

had gained some rest and
sleep and are ready to
go in and try their chances
with the "Army of Northern
Va" and again try their hand.
In the middle of the P.M.
the battle commenced raging
with fearful loss of life
on both sides. hour after hour
the battle rolled on with
a great deal anxiety as
to how the tide would
go but before sun set
the odds was consider
able in our favor. Among
the badly wounded was
Genl's Sickels & Hancock
the former loosing the
right leg above the Knee
the latter tho not seri
ly wounded lost much

Memorandum of Events
which transpir while
Campaining in Va during
the summer months of
1863.

July 1st 1863 The great
battle of Gettys burg Pa
commenced, at the close
of the day the field was
held by the enemy, a large
number of Prisioners were
captured mostly of 1st Corps
Genl Reynolds fell during
the first part of the engagement
the 1st and 11nd sustained
the whole loss. At Sun
set the 12th 2nd and 3d
which had marched at least
18 miles came up & were
thrown in line of Battle
on the morning of the 2nd

DIARIES
These diaries were written by Doctor Tarbell between 1861 and 1865. They provide descriptions of Army life and Tarbell's experiences in combat, including a detailed account of the Battle of Gettysburg. (*Tompkins County History Center*)

LETTER, APRIL 6, 1865 FROM
DOCTOR TARBELL TO HIS WIFE, MARY
More than one hundred of their letters have survived.
(Tompkins County History Center)

PEWTER MESS KIT
This mess kit was used by Doctor Tarbell during his military service.
(Tompkins County History Center)

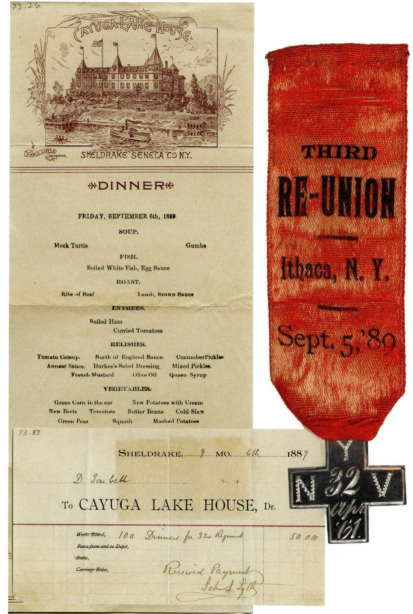

DINNER MENU, RECEIPT AND RIBBON
From a reunion dinner of Tarbell's regiment, the 32nd New York
Volunteer Infantry. (Tompkins County History Center)

The Telegraph in the Civil War

New York University professor Samuel Morse developed the telegraph in 1835 and secured a patent in 1840. The telegraph quickly revolutionized communication in the United States and abroad.

During the Civil War, the North's well-developed system of telegraph lines made it possible for the Lincoln administration to oversee the war effort and for Grant to implement his continental strategy. The telegraph also enabled Northerners to follow wartime events as they happened.

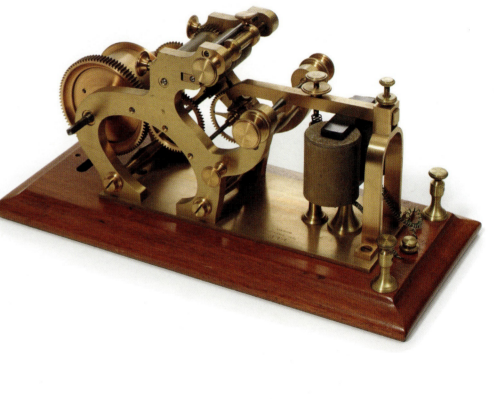

TELEGRAPH SOUNDER
Civil War–era telegraph sounder from the railroad depot at Elmira, New York. *(Chemung County Historical Society)*

TELEGRAPH RECORDER
Civil War–era telegraph recorder.
(New York State Museum Collection, H-1943.8.1)

THE ARMY TELEGRAPH
The invention of the telegraph enabled leaders in Washington to communicate quickly with armies in the field.
Harper's Weekly, January 24, 1863 *(New York State Library, Manuscripts and Special Collections)*

On To Richmond

By 1864, Lincoln had unified command of Northern armies under Ulysses S. Grant. He directed William Tecumseh Sherman's western armies to swing through Georgia and the Carolinas, while the Army of the Potomac relentlessly pursued General Lee's army through Virginia. Grant viewed destroying Lee's army as the key to victory. It was, in effect, the anvil on which Sherman would strike the hammer blow. *Harper's Weekly,* June 18, 1864 *(New York State Library, Manuscripts and Special Collections)*

On To Richmond!
(1864–1865)

As 1864 began, the North brought its industrial might and superior resources to bear on the South. The Union Navy's blockade choked off supplies, and Union armies overwhelmed Southern industrial centers. New Yorkers, weary from three years of war, joined other Americans in debating the war's conduct during a critical presidential election.

U.S. armies ended the Southern rebellion in the spring of 1865—after four years of the costliest war Americans had ever endured. But the nation's rejoicing was soon tempered by the assassination of its greatest president. New Yorkers joined their fellow countrymen in mourning Abraham Lincoln and setting the nation on a new course.

Battle of the Wilderness

In May 1864, Lee sought to surprise Grant and the Army of the Potomac near Chancellorsville, Virginia. Several hours of intense fighting in heavily wooded terrain produced 17,000 Union and 10,000 Confederate casualties. Despite the defeat, Grant did not retreat but pressed on toward Richmond and kept Lee on the defensive.

OUR WOUNDED ESCAPING FROM THE FIRES IN THE WILDERNESS
During the battle, the dry brush in the area caught fire, creating an inferno from which the wounded could not escape. *Harper's Weekly,* June 4, 1864 *(New York State Library, Manuscripts and Special Collections)*

43rd New York Volunteer Infantry

The 43rd New York Volunteers were heavily involved in the fighting at the Battle of the Wilderness. Forty-three men were killed, ninety-four were wounded, and another sixty-one listed as missing. Among those killed were Colonel John Wilson, Lieutenant Colonel John Fryer, and Major William Wallace.

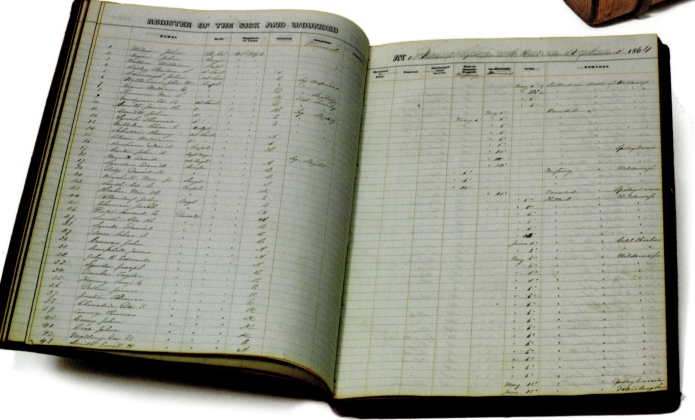

SUITCASE
This suitcase belonged to Lieutenant Colonel John Fryer, killed during the Battle of the Wilderness.
(New York State Museum Collection, H-1972.37.7)

LEDGER BOOK
This ledger was kept by the regimental hospital for the 43rd New York Volunteers. This page shows Wilson, Fryer, and Wallace as men killed during the Battle of the Wilderness.
(New York State Museum Collection, H-1990.36.1)

COLONEL JOHN WILSON
A resolution from the Albany Common
Council: "Resolved, That in his death our
country has lost one of her most earnest,
faithful defenders, our city one of its brightest
ornaments, his widowed mother a most dutiful
son, and his weeping sisters a loving brother."
(New York State Museum Collection, H-1962.9.8)

LIEUTENANT COLONEL JOHN FRYER
From a resolution adopted by the Citizens of
Greenbush: "Resolved, That in his death his
parents are called upon to mourn the loss of
a dutiful son, his sisters an affectionate brother,
his friends a worthy companion, and his
country a tried and true defender."
(New York State Museum Collection, H-1962.9.10)

MAJOR WILLIAM WALLACE
From a resolution adopted by the Albany
Typographical Union No. 4: "Resolved, That
by his death our country has lost an ardent
defender—our city a public-spirited and
honorable citizen, and our Society an energetic
and useful member."
(New York State Museum Collection, H-1962.9.9)

General Philip H. Sheridan (1831–1888)

Philip Sheridan—who claimed to have been born in Albany—was one of the Union's most distinguished generals. General Grant gave him command of the Army of the Potomac's cavalry corps. Sheridan gained fame for defeating the Confederate army in the Shenandoah Valley and halting the last significant Rebel invasion of the North. In so doing, he implemented a scorched earth policy—and brought the war to the civilian population—to prevent the valley's crops from being used to feed Southern troops.

PHOTOGRAPH
The son of Irish immigrants, Philip Sheridan attended the United States Military Academy at West Point and graduated in 1854. *(New York State Library, Manuscripts and Special Collections)*

PORTRAIT
General Philip H. Sheridan, oil on canvas, by Daniel Huntington (1874). *(New York State Museum Collection, H-2003.41.76)*

SHERIDAN'S RIDE

On October 19, 1864, Confederate General Jubal Early launched an attack on Sheridan's force along Cedar Creek in Virginia. General Sheridan was in Winchester, Virginia—about fifteen miles away—when news of the fighting arrived. In his legendary ride, Sheridan arrived on the scene in time to organize his defenses and launch a counterattack that routed Early's army and ended the threat to the Shenandoah Valley. *(New York State Military Museum, Division of Military and Naval Affairs)*

121st New York Volunteer Infantry

"Upton's Regulars"

The 121st New York Volunteer Infantry Regiment was raised in Oswego and Herkimer Counties. Following the Battle of Antietam, the regiment was commanded by Emory Upton of Batavia, Genesee County. The men earned a reputation for hard fighting in virtually every battle fought by the Army of the Potomac.

Emory Upton and his men helped to develop new tactics for assaulting Confederate entrenchments around Petersburg, Virginia, that would remain Army doctrine through World War I.

SHERIDAN'S ARMY MARCHES THROUGH THE SHENANDOAH
The 121st New York and other veteran regiments of the Army of the Potomac were rushed to Washington to confront the Confederate raid in Maryland. After defeating General Jubal Early in the Shenandoah Valley, the 121st returned to the Army of the Potomac and was instrumental in the final assault on Petersburg.
(New York State Library, Manuscripts and Special Collections)

CAP BOX, BAYONET, AND SCABBARD
Accoutrements from a soldier in the 121st New York Volunteers. This regiment was part of General Sheridan's army during the Shenandoah Valley Campaign. During the Battle of Cedar Creek, ten men of the 121st New York were killed and forty-two wounded. Its total loss of 839 men killed or wounded was among the highest of any regiment during the war. *(New York State Museum Collection, H-1971.91.7 A-D)*

The Battle for Atlanta and Sherman's March to the Sea

General William Tecumseh Sherman broke the back of the Confederacy in 1864. After taking charge of Union troops in the West, he engaged in a series of battles in Georgia before capturing the railroad hub of Atlanta in September. Sherman's army then laid waste to the countryside, devastating both military and civilian populations on its march to the Atlantic. After capturing Savannah in December, Sherman marched north, planning to join forces with General Grant in Virginia.

LESLIE'S ILLUSTRATED, JANUARY 14, 1865
After capturing Atlanta, General Sherman ordered all civilians evacuated before ordering the city to be burned. (*New York State Library, Manuscripts and Special Collections*)

MURAL, "THE BATTLE OF RESACA"

Confederate General Joseph Johnston had fought a defensive retreat, hoping that weariness of the war would lead to President Lincoln's defeat in the 1864 election. In July, Johnston was replaced by General John B. Hood, a more aggressive commander, who attempted to meet Sherman's army in open battle. Hood's defeat outside Atlanta forced him to abandon the Confederacy's second largest industrial center.
(New York State Military Museum, Division of Military and Naval Affairs)

BATTERY I FLAG

This flag was presented to Battery I, 1st New York Artillery, in March 1864 by "friends of the battery." The battery was known as "Weidrich's Battery." The buffalo at center of the flag symbolizes the men's hometown.
(New York State Military Museum, Division of Military and Naval Affairs)

Lieutenant Colonel Michael Weidrich (1820–1899)

Michael Weidrich, a recent immigrant from Alsace-Lorraine, commanded an artillery battery with Buffalo's 1st New York Volunteer Artillery. Weidrich and his men initially saw combat in the east at the Battles of Cross Keys, Second Bull Run, Chancellorsville, and Gettysburg.

Afterward, the 1st Artillery was transferred to the west and served with Sherman on his March to the Sea. In March 1864, Weidrich was promoted to command of the 15th New York Heavy Artillery for the remainder of the war.

SWORD AND SHOULDER STRAPS
This presentation sword was given to Lieutenant Colonel Weidrich by the citizens of Buffalo. The shoulder straps reflect his rank as a lieutenant colonel after he took command of the 15th New York Heavy Artillery. *(Buffalo History Museum)*

MICHAEL WEIDRICH
Brevet Colonel Michael Weidrich as commander of the 15th New York Heavy Artillery.
(New York State Military Museum, Division of Military and Naval Affairs)

185

The Election of 1864

Although Abraham Lincoln won a landslide victory in the presidential election of 1864, his re-election was anything but assured. As the war dragged into its fourth year, Americans were divided, and Lincoln faced a strong challenge from Democrat and former Union General George B. McClellan. Radical Republicans were also contesting his candidacy. The president needed a military victory to win public support, and General Sherman provided it with his September capture of Atlanta. Lincoln ended up carrying all but three states—but he only won New York by a margin of less than one percent.

CARD
This card features a political cartoon titled, "The Platforms as Interpreted by the Soldiers." Many Northern states, including New York, permitted soldiers serving in the field to vote in the election of 1864—a first. Lincoln garnered over 70 percent of the soldiers' votes. (*New York State Museum Collection, H-1981.61.1*)

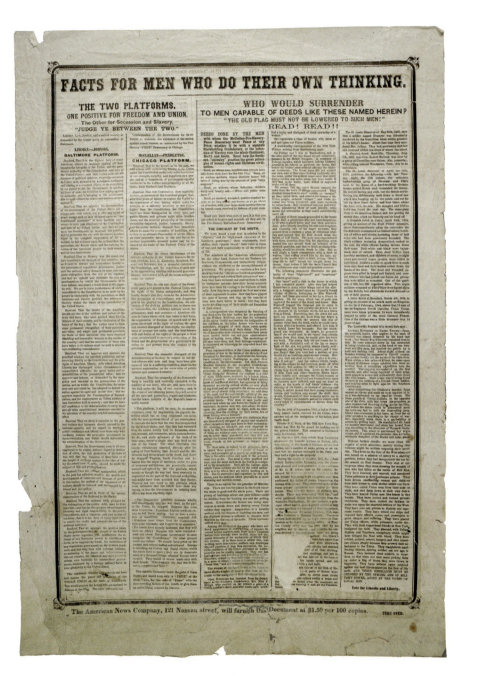

186

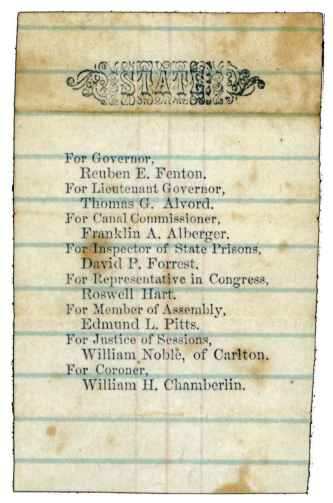

BALLOT
New York State election ballot for 1864.
(New York State Museum Collection, H-2006.71.47)

BROADSIDE, FACTS FOR MEN WHO DO THEIR OWN THINKING: THE
TWO PLATFORMS, ONE POSITIVE FOR FREEDOM AND UNION, THE
OTHER FOR SECESSION AND SLAVERY, *left*
Pro-Republican broadside from the election of 1864. During the
campaign of 1864, President Lincoln's reelection was far from certain.
(New York State Library, Manuscripts and Special Collections)

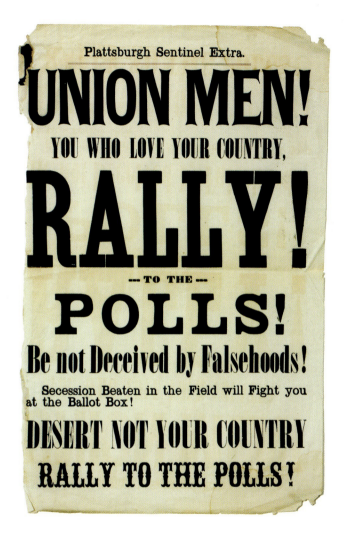

RALLY! TO THE POLLS!
This 1864 Pro-Republican broadside from Plattsburgh, Clinton County,
calls on New Yorkers to save the Union by going to the ballot box. The
Democratic Candidate, General George McClellan, was running on a
platform that called for an end to the fighting and, potentially, recognition
of an independent Confederate States of America.
(New York State Museum Collection, H-1976.191.4)

187

Reuben E. Fenton (1819–1885)

Republican Reuben E. Fenton replaced Democrat Horatio Seymour as governor of New York in 1864. A native of Chautauqua County, Fenton opposed slavery while serving in the U.S. Congress before the war. He was an early supporter of the Republican Party and even chaired the state's first Republican Convention. When peace was restored, Fenton became an advocate for veterans' rights, public education, and public health. He served until 1868, when he was elected to the U.S. Senate. As a senator, he supported a moderate Republican agenda and backed Horace Greeley over Ulysses S. Grant in the 1872 presidential election.

The Fall of Charleston

The capture of Savannah provided the North with a wonderful Christmas gift. In the New Year, Sherman turned north and invaded the Carolinas in a push to unite with Grant in Virginia, trapping Robert E. Lee between two armies. Union forces had attempted to capture Charleston, South Carolina, since 1863. It was finally captured in early 1865. Many in the North regarded the city as the birthplace of secession.

PORTRAIT
Fenton's first piece of legislation as a congressman was a bill to grant relief to invalid veterans of the American Revolution and the War of 1812. His concern for the welfare of veterans would distinguish his career as governor. (*New York State Library, Manuscripts and Special Collections*)

NOS. 165, 167 AND 169 MEETING STREET, CHARLESTON, S. C.

EAST BAY STREET, LOOKING SOUTH.

KITCHEN ATTACHED TO 53 WENTWORTH STREET—EFFECT OF TWO SHELLS.

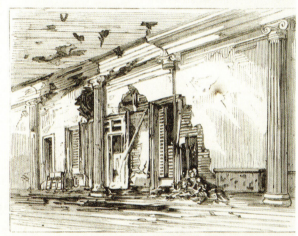

GENTLEMEN'S ORDINARY, CHARLESTON HOTEL.

THE PRESENT APPEARANCE
OF CHARLESTON
Much of the city was left in
ruins after years of artillery
barrages. *Leslie's Illustrated*,
March 25, 1865
*(New York State Library,
Manuscripts and Special
Collections)*

James N. McGregor (1830–1894)

Born in Oyster Bay, Nassau County, James McGregor enlisted in August 1862. By 1865, the 127th was assigned to General Sherman's Army as it marched north from Savannah into the Carolinas. On February 18, 1865, Confederate troops evacuated Charleston, and the city surrendered to Sherman. The 127th New York was assigned to garrison duty in Charleston for the remainder of the war. McGregor, a farmer by trade, survived the war and raised his family in Connecticut.

The Siege of Petersburg

In June 1864, the Union Army suffered a defeat at Cold Harbor, Virginia, that prevented General Grant from marching directly on Richmond. Instead, he turned to the railroad and supply center of Petersburg, twenty-five miles south of the Rebel capital. Grant correctly understood that he could force the Confederates to abandon Richmond by capturing Petersburg. After failing to overrun Petersburg on June 15, 1864, Grant laid siege to the city. The Confederates held on for 292 days, but finally had to abandon the city on April 2, 1865.

NINTH ARMY CORPS CHARGING THE CONFEDERATE WORKS BEFORE PETERSBURG, *right*
Frank Leslie's Illustrated drawing of the Union assault immediately after the detonation of the mine. When Union troops charged into the crater caused by the explosion, they became victims of what Confederate General Mahone described as a "turkey shoot."
Leslies's Illustrated 1864
(New York State Library, Manuscripts and Special Collections)

SWORD
This sword belonged to James McGregor of the 127th New York Volunteers. *(The Philip Brown Collection)*

THE NINTH ARMY CORPS CHARGING THE CONFEDERATE WORKS, BEFORE PETERSBURG, IMMEDIATELY AFTER THE EXPLOSION OF THE MINE, JUNE 30TH, 1864.

THE CRATER, *left*

In June 1864, Union engineers dug a mine beneath Confederate trenches and detonated gunpowder that they hoped would blow a hole in the Rebel lines. The explosion created a massive crater and killed nearly three hundred Confederates. The Rebels recovered and drove back Union attackers—which included a division of African American troops under the command of General Edward Ferrero of New York City. Union losses were twice as high as those of the Confederates.
(The Photographic History of the Civil War in Ten Volumes, New York, 1911)

THE FINAL NIGHT ASSAULT ON PETERSBURG

Frank Leslie's Illustrated drawing depicting one of the repeated Union assaults on the Confederate fortifications at Petersburg.
Leslie's Illustrated, April 22, 1865
(New York State Library, Manuscripts and Special Collections)

8-INCH SIEGE MORTAR
(Library of Congress)

FINAL BATTLES AROUND PETERSBURG, *left*
New York printmakers Currier & Ives depict one of the final battles around Petersburg in this print. Unlike many of their earlier works, individuals are subsumed by the anonymity of the mass of humanity that the Civil War armies had become by 1865.
(Library of Congress)

MODEL 1841 8-INCH COEHORN MORTAR
As the Union Army tightened its grip around Petersburg, mortars of various sizes were used to lob explosive shells into the Rebel defenses. During the siege of Petersburg, Union artillerymen fired approximately 40,000 mortar shells into Confederate lines. This Coehorn mortar has an 8 inch bore, and it fired a 44 pound shell. This "light" mortar—920 pounds—was designed for use in the trenches during a siege.
(New York State Military Museum, Division of Military and Naval Affairs)

CARTE DE VISITE, MESS SET, POCKET WATCH, CORPS BADGE, CANTEEN, SWORD, AND DIARIES
These personal effects were carried by William McCormack, 91st New York Volunteers. The regiment was raised in the Capital Region and spent much of the war in Louisiana. In 1865, the 91st returned to the Eastern Theater and fought in the Battle of Five Forks. Known as "the Waterloo of the Confederacy," this battle ended the siege of Petersburg. William McCormack's diaries record his wartime experiences from 1863–65. The entry shown here, dated April 1, 1865, describes preparations for the Union assault at Five Forks during the Siege of Petersburg. The Union Army of the Civil War was the most literate army ever fielded. Soldiers of all ranks penned countless diaries and letters that are a trove of information about all aspects of the conflict. *(New York State Museum Collection, H 1949.1.1–.10C)*

The Fall of Richmond, Virginia

The Confederates abandoned Richmond—their capital—when Petersburg fell. Union troops entered the city on April 3, 1865; only hours after the president of the Confederacy, Jefferson Davis, had fled. Two officers of the 13th New York Artillery raised the first American flag to fly over Richmond in nearly four years. Despite the loss of their capital, the Confederates continued to fight—as did General Grant, who was more interested in defeating Lee's army than occupying the Confederate capital.

UNION TROOPS ENTERING RICHMOND ON APRIL 3, 1865
Frank Leslie's Illustrated, April 29, 1865 *(New York State Library, Manuscripts and Special Collections)*

Appomattox Courthouse

Grant's army pursued Lee as he retreated from Petersburg. The two armies engaged in a series of running battles, but when General Sheridan's troops raced ahead and entrenched themselves across Lee's line of retreat, Lee made the decision to offer his unconditional surrender to Grant. The two met at Appomattox Courthouse, Virginia, on April 9, 1865, and effectively ended the war.

NEW YORK CELEBRATES
Nearly four years after the firing on Fort Sumter, war-weary New Yorkers were finally able to celebrate their country's victory. Lee's surrender of the Confederates' largest army did not officially end the war—the last Rebel field army would not surrender until June 23, in Texas—but it was clear that it was only a matter of time until the last Rebel soldiers would lay down their arms.
Leslie's Illustrated, April 22, 1865
(New York State Library, Manuscripts and Special Collections)

LEE'S SURRENDER

This print depicts generals Ulysses S. Grant and Robert E. Lee discussing the terms of Lee's surrender at the McLean House in Appomattox Courthouse, Virginia. General Ely S. Parker, who drafted the terms, is shown standing fifth from the right. *(Library of Congress)*

General Ely S. Parker (1828–1895)

Born at Indian Falls on the Tonawanda Reservation, Genesee County, Ely S. Parker was a Seneca chief who became General Grant's aide-de-camp, first in the Western Theater and then after Grant was named General in Chief. As such, Parker wrote out the terms of surrender at Appomattox. Before the war, Parker was an attorney, engineer, and diplomat for the Seneca Nation. Afterward, Grant made him the first Native American to serve as commissioner of the Office of Indian Affairs.

Ely S. Parker
Ely S. Parker drafted the terms of surrender that General Grant presented to Robert E. Lee on April 9, 1865.
(New York State Museum Ethnology Collections)

PRESIDENT LINCOLN RIDING THROUGH RICHMOND
New York's *Frank Leslie's Illustrated* celebrated the fall of the Confederate capital by depicting a triumphant President Lincoln being thronged by those he had set free through his Emancipation Proclamation. Due to the delay in reporting, this edition was published one week after the President was assassinated.
Frank Leslie's Illustrated, April 22, 1865 (*New York State Library, Manuscripts and Special Collections*)

Booth.   Mr. Lincoln.   Mrs. Lincoln.   Miss Harris.   Major Rathbun.

ASSASSINATION OF PRESIDENT LINCOLN IN HIS PRIVATE BOX AT FORD'S THEATER, WASHINGTON, APRIL 14.

The National Calamity

On April 14, just five days after Lee's surrender, Confederate sympathizer John Wilkes Booth shot President Lincoln in Ford's Theater in Washington, D.C. Lincoln was carried to a nearby boarding house where he died early the next morning. As part of the conspiracy to kill the three highest ranking U.S. officials on the same day, Lewis Powell broke into Secretary of State William Seward's home and badly wounded him. Seward survived the attack. A third co-conspirator, George Atzerodt, was to murder Vice President Andrew Johnson, but fled the capital.

. . . O Captain! my Captain! rise up and hear the bells;

Rise up—for you the flag is flung—for you the bugle trills;

For you bouquets and ribboned wreaths—for you the shores a-crowding;

For you they call, the swaying mass, their eager faces turning . . .

—*Walt Whitman, "O Captain! My Captain!" 1865*

THE ASSASSINATION OF LINCOLN
John Wilkes Booth despised Lincoln for his Emancipation Proclamation. Booth hoped that Lincoln's death would enable the Confederacy to rally and continue the war. After shooting President Lincoln, John Wilkes Booth leapt onto the stage and shouted, "Sic Semper Tyrannis"—"Thus always to Tyrants"—and fled the theater.
(New York State Library, Manuscripts and Special Collections)

Clara Harris and Henry Reed Rathbone

When General Ulysses S. Grant and his wife were unable to attend Ford's Theater, the Lincolns invited Clara Harris, the daughter of New York Senator Ira Harris and a friend of Mrs. Lincoln's, and her fiancé, Major Henry Rathbone. Rathbone, a veteran of the war, struggled with John Wilkes Booth and suffered severe knife wounds before Booth made his escape.

MAJOR HENRY RATHBONE
Albany native Henry Rathbone, who was seated with the Lincolns at Ford's Theater, struggled with John Wilkes Booth after the shooting. Booth was only able to escape after stabbing Rathbone.
(New York State Library, Manuscripts and Special Collections)

CLARA HARRIS
Clara Harris accompanied President and Mrs. Lincoln to Ford's Theater on the evening of April 14, 1865.
(New York State Library, Manuscripts and Special Collections)

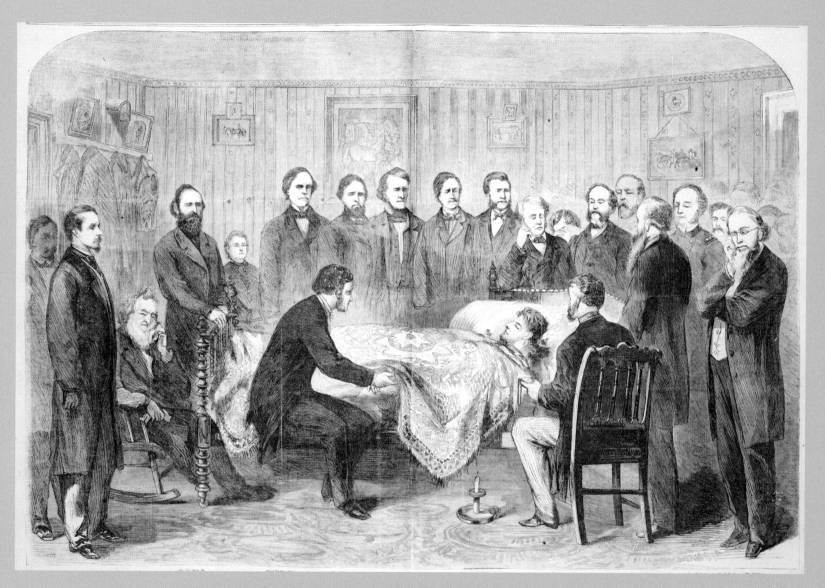

LINCOLN'S DYING MOMENTS
President Lincoln was rushed from Ford's Theater and taken to a nearby boarding house
where he was treated by doctors. He died in the early morning hours of April 15, 1865.
Leslie's Illustrated, April 29, 1865 *(New York State Library, Manuscripts and Special Collections)*

SERGEANT BOSTON CORBETT
16th New York Volunteer Cavalry
(New York State Library, Manuscripts and Special Collections)

THE KILLING OF BOOTH BY BOSTON CORBETT *(right)*
On April 26, after a 12-day manhunt, soldiers of the 16th New York Volunteer Cavalry caught up with Booth near Garrett Farm in Port Royal, Virginia. After a brief standoff, Booth was shot and killed by Sergeant Boston Corbett of Troy, Rensselaer County.
Leslie's Illustrated, May 13, 1865
(New York State Library, Manuscripts and Special Collections)

JOHN WILKES BOOTH
John Wilkes Booth despised Lincoln for his Emancipation Proclamation. Booth hoped that Lincoln's death would enable the Confederacy to rally and emerge victorious.
(New York State Library, Manuscripts and Special Collections)

207

The Funeral Train

After a state funeral in the nation's capital, the president's body traveled to Springfield, Illinois, to be laid to rest. Millions of grief-stricken Americans viewed the funeral train as it retraced the path of President-elect Lincoln's 1861 inaugural train.

The funeral train operated with military efficiency and made stops in twelve cities—including New York, Albany, and Buffalo. Mourners waited to glimpse the train as it passed through more than four hundred communities along the route.

ROSETTES AND BADGES
These rosettes and badges were worn by grieving New Yorkers during the funeral programs for President Lincoln.
(New York State Military Museum, Division of Military and Naval Affairs)

RIFLE
This Patrick Smith–manufactured rifle was carried by a member of the Union Continentals, a Buffalo home guard unit which served as the honor guard for the fallen president. The Continentals—formed and commanded by former president Millard Fillmore—had served as Lincoln's escort during his inaugural procession.
(New York State Museum Collection, H-1973.107.1)

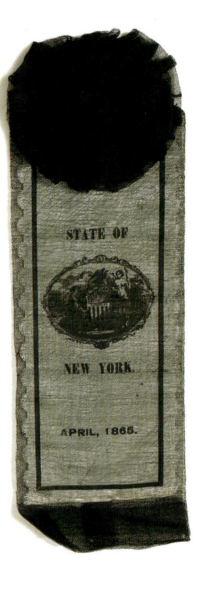

CITY HALL, NEW YORK CITY, *right*
Crowd waiting to view Lincoln's body at City Hall in New York City.
(New York State Library, Manuscripts and Special Collections)

THE NATION MOURNS.

FUNERAL PROCESSION
New York's own "inner civil war" remained unresolved as Lincoln's funeral procession made its way along Fifth Avenue. African American troops who requested to be included in the procession were forced to march at the rear of the column.
(New York State Library, Manuscripts and Special Collections)

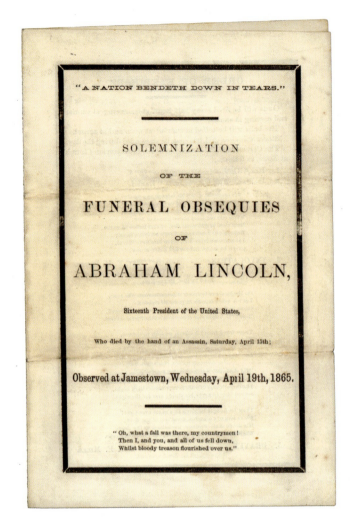

"A NATION BENDETH DOWN IN TEARS."

SOLEMNIZATION

OF THE

FUNERAL OBSEQUIES

OF

ABRAHAM LINCOLN,

Sixteenth President of the United States,

Who died by the hand of an Assassin, Saturday, April 15th;

Observed at Jamestown, Wednesday, April 19th, 1865.

"Oh, what a fall was there, my countrymen!
Then I, and you, and all of us fell down,
Whilst bloody treason flourished over us."

FUNERAL OBSEQUIES
Program detailing funerary events for President Lincoln in Jamestown, New York. *(New York State Museum Collection, H-1976.256.1)*

DOWNTOWN ALBANY DRAPED IN BLACK, *right*
Downtown Albany draped in black during President Lincoln's funeral. The view was taken looking up State Street from Broadway.
(Albany Institute of History & Art)

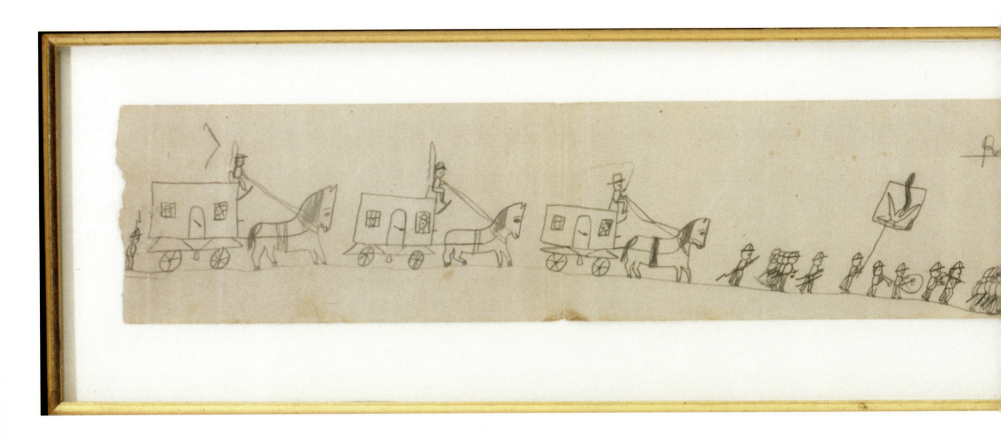

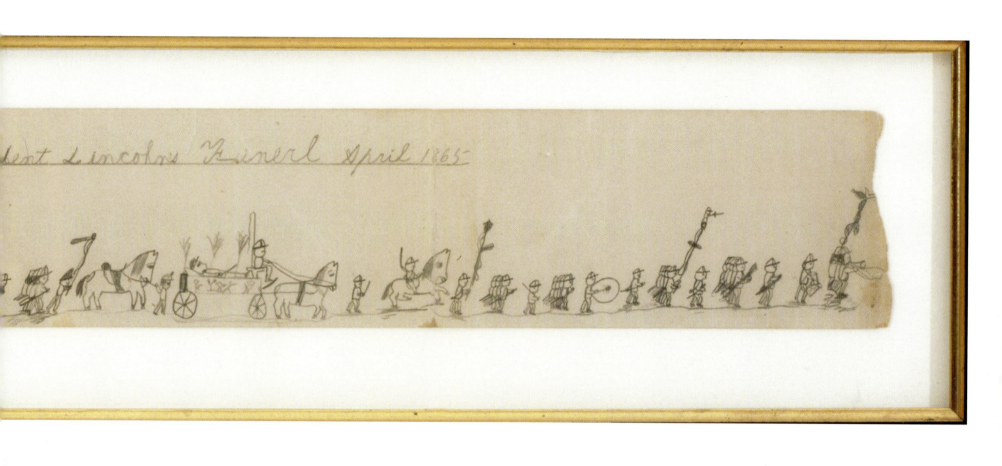

...ent Lincolns Funerl April 1865

Child's Drawing

Julian DeVaux O'Brien, the nine-year-old son of John A. and Caroline O'Brien witnessed and recorded Abraham Lincoln's funeral procession in Albany, April 25, 1865. His father was a dealer in millinery goods at 45 N. Pearl Street from 1857 through 1876. The O'Brien family resided at 101 Clinton Avenue.

(Albany Institute of History & Art)

213

LETTER

This letter from thirteen-year-old Wesley Griffin to his brother in the Union Army, details the public viewing of President Lincoln's casket at the New York State Capitol in Albany. Wesley waited in line four times to view the President's coffin.

(William F. Howard Collection)

Reconstruction and Legacy

Jennifer A. Lemak, Robert Weible

By the end of the Civil War, 448,000 New Yorkers had enlisted in the armed services, and more than 50,000 of them had died. While the cost of the war was terribly high, New Yorkers and other Americans had preserved their democratic union. And 4,000,000 people had won their freedom. Afterwards, New Yorkers and other Americans recovered from the war and commemorated it while forever contesting its memory.

"Soldiers, your state thanks you and gives you a pledge of her lasting gratitude."

—*Governor Reuben Fenton on the occasion of the presentation of regimental flags, April 1865*

THE TRIUMPH IN NEW YORK
This was the scene in New York City's Central Park as the war drew to a close and soldiers returned home in March 1865.
(Lee Foundation)

Returned Volunteer/How the Fort Was Taken, JOHN ROGERS, 1864, PLASTER

The triumphant Union soldier returning from war was one of John Rogers's most famous Civil War subjects. This statue stayed in the artist's sales catalog until 1889, long after the other Civil War subjects were discontinued.

(New York State Museum Collection, H-1979.182.1)

CIVIL WAR VETERAN, *right*

Robert M. Round, Civil War veteran from Ripley, Chautauqua County. In 1935 at the age of 92, Round was elected as Commander of the State Department of the G.A.R.

(New York State Archives)

Returning Home

As the armies disbanded, New York's volunteer soldiers returned home to a country that had been forever changed. In 1866, Union veterans formed the Grand Army of the Republic (G.A.R.) in Decatur, Illinois. Local posts sprouted up all over the country, with 676 in New York alone. At first, the G.A.R. supported the political goals of the Republican Party, but by the mid-1870s, it began advocating more narrowly for pensions and veterans' rights. The G.A.R. reached its nationwide peak of half-a-million members in the 1890s. It dissolved in 1956 when its last member died.

For many Union veterans, the war had initially been an adventure. Illusions were shattered as the war dragged on, however, and soldiers faced losses and horrors they could never have imagined. Thousands bore the scars of battle, while others carried wounds that left no marks. Some returning veterans consequently needed long-term care that was more than their families and friends could provide.

The State of New York recognized its need to care for its veterans in 1872 when it passed legislation to construct the New York State Soldiers' and Sailors' Home in Bath, Steuben County—with $100,000 in funds raised by the G.A.R.. Work on the Home began in June 1877, and the facility opened on Christmas Day 1878. Its campus-like environment included a hospital ward, dining hall, stage, store, and recreation area. It housed between 1,100 and 2,150 residents at any given time from the 1890s through the 1910s. In 1930, ownership of the Home was transferred to the federal government's newly formed Veterans Administration.

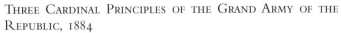

THREE CARDINAL PRINCIPLES OF THE GRAND ARMY OF THE
REPUBLIC, 1884
The three principles of the G.A.R. were loyalty, fraternity, and
charity. The G.A.R. became one of the first organized advocacy
groups in American politics. *(Library of Congress)*

WHEELCHAIR, C.1890
This wheelchair was used at the Bath Soldiers' and Sailors' Home. It
was probably a resident's personal chair since there are no handles to
push the chair from behind. *(Edwin Presley)*

BARRACKS A, B, AND C AT THE NEW YORK STATE SOLDIERS' AND SAILORS' HOME IN BATH, STEUBEN COUNTY, 1897
(New York State Library)

THE CANTEEN ON THE GROUNDS OF THE NEW YORK STATE SOLDIERS' AND SAILORS' HOME, 1897
(New York State Library)

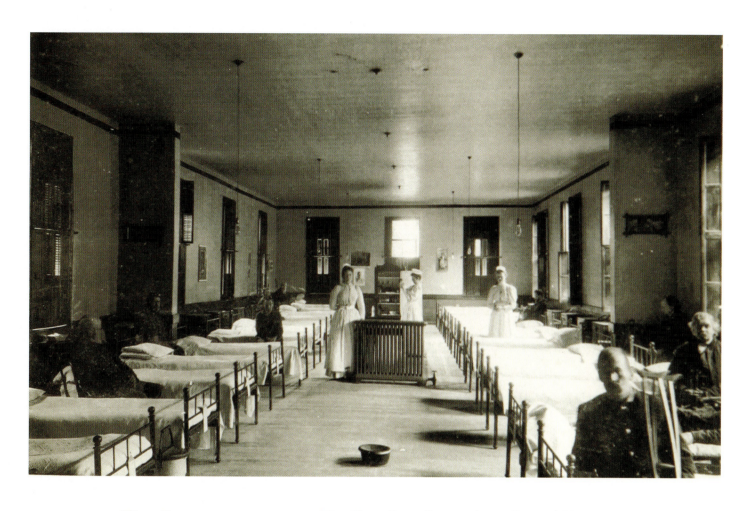

WARD F IN THE HOSPITAL AT THE NEW YORK STATE SOLDIERS' AND SAILORS' HOME, 1897
(New York State Library)

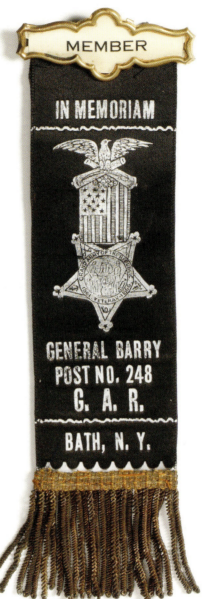

MENU, 1911
This booklet is a menu for the 1911 Christmas celebration at the Soldiers' and Sailors' Home. Residents enjoyed a dinner of roast turkey, dressing, sweet potatoes, peas, corn, pickled beets, and plum pudding with brandy sauce. *(Robert Yott)*

RIBBON, FRONT AND BACK, C.1895
The General Barry Post 248 G.A.R. was made up entirely from residents living at the Bath Soldiers' and Sailors' Home. *(Robert Yott)*

SOUVENIR PLATE, CHINA, C. 1930
The Bath Soldiers' Monument depicted on this plate was erected in 1883 at the cost of $4,000 raised through public subscription.
(Robert Yott)

SOUVENIR SPOON, C. 1900
This spoon depicts the main building of the Soldiers' and Sailors' Home. Souvenir spoons were popular in the 1900s and were collected as trophies of places a person visited.
(Robert Yott)

KNIFE, C. 1900
This knife was made for and used in the Soldiers' and Sailors' Home. The handle is labeled with the initials: *N.Y.S.S. & S. HOME.*
(Robert Yott)

PHOTOGRAPH OF BROMLEY HOKE, C.1880
In an era where exclusion and segregation were widespread, the G.A.R. often welcomed both black and white veterans. These materials belonged to Bromley Hoke, who was an active G.A.R. member.
(New York State Museum Collection, H-2006.60.1)

Bromley Hoke (1847–1913) was a farm laborer in Canajoharie, Montgomery County, before he enlisted with the Massachusetts 54th Infantry Regiment in April 1863 at age 16. The Massachusetts 54th was one of the first official African American units in the Civil War. Hoke served with the 54th until June 16, 1865, when he received a disability discharge. Upon returning to Canajoharie, Hoke joined the G.A.R., found work at the Wagner Hotel as a waiter, and married Elizabeth 'Lizzie' Ann Philips in 1893. The couple lived the remainder of their lives in Canajoharie.

BROMLEY HOKE, CALLING CARD WITH G.A.R. INSIGNIA, UNIFORM FRAGMENT, AND SMALL SWORD HAT DECORATION
(New York State Library, Manuscripts and Special Collections)

Ribbons belonging to Bromley Hoke who was active in the G.A.R. until his death in 1913

Massachusetts 54th Ribbon, c.1870. The Massachusetts 54th was one of the first official black units in the Civil War; hundreds of black New Yorkers volunteered to serve in it. *(New York State Museum Collection, H-2006.60.7)*

Badge: "Robert A. Bell, Post No. 134, 24th National Encampment, Aug. 12th, 1890, Boston, Mass." *(New York State Library, Manuscripts and Special Collections)*

Badge: "New York, 41st National Encampment, Saratoga Springs, September 1907" *(New York State Library, Manuscripts and Special Collections)*

Badge: "Grand Army of the Republic. In Memoriam, U.S. Grant, Post No. 5, Philadelphia" *(New York State Library, Manuscripts and Special Collections)*

Reconstruction

After the war, the United States government attempted to bring former Confederate states back into the Union by "reconstructing" Southern society. Lincoln's successor, Andrew Johnson, favored a conservative course of action. Radical Republicans, on the other hand, aggressively promoted civil rights by enfranchising African Americans, building public schools in the South, and modernizing the Southern economy. Southerners resisted the government's efforts, often violently, and Northern backers of Reconstruction abandoned their cause in 1877. Republicans agreed to withdraw federal troops from the South in exchange for Democrats' willingness to support the 1876 presidential election of Rutherford B. Hayes over New York's Governor Samuel J. Tilden.

Radical Republicans had envisioned the transformation of a slave society into a free one. Their amendments to the Constitution, passed during Reconstruction, laid the groundwork for the Civil Rights movement of the 1960s. The Thirteenth Amendment (1865) abolished slavery. The Fourteenth (1868) granted citizenship to African Americans. The Fifteenth (1870) granted voting rights regardless of "race, color, or previous condition of servitude."

"THIS IS A WHITE MAN'S GOVERNMENT."
The Civil War abolished slavery, but racial prejudice thrived in both the North and the South. This 1868 political cartoon by Thomas Nast depicts three Democrats: an Irishman, Ku Klux Klan founder Nathan Bedford Forrest, and Wall Street financier August Belmont standing atop a black veteran while the Colored Orphan Asylum burns in the background. Democrats capitalized on anti-black sentiment to garner support from the working classes. (Library of Congress)

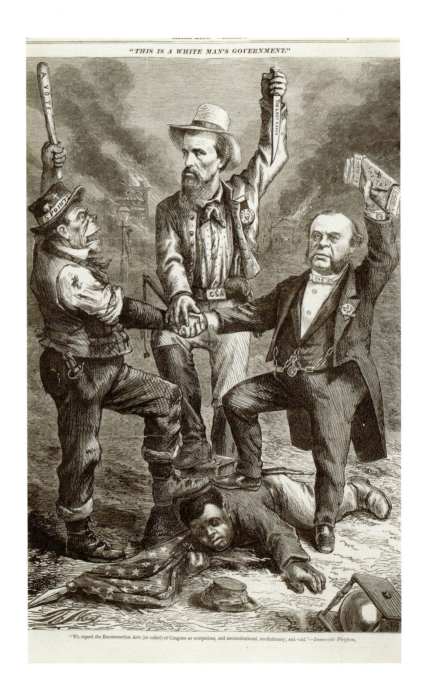

"THIS IS A WHITE MAN'S GOVERNMENT."

"We regard the Reconstruction Acts (so called) of Congress as usurpations, and unconstitutional, revolutionary, and void."—*Democratic Platform.*

THE FIFTEENTH AMENDMENT

This image depicts a parade celebrating the passage of the 15th Amendment surrounded by portraits and vignettes of African Americans excising their newly won liberties—land ownership, education, political involvement, religious freedom, employment, and military participation. *(Library of Congress)*

The Fifteenth Amendment affected New Yorkers as well as former slave states. By mandating universal black male suffrage, the amendment thwarted New Yorkers who had previously voted against black voting rights in 1840, 1846, and 1869.

During his presidency (1869–1877), General Ulysses S. Grant supported Reconstruction and enforced civil rights laws.

Running against former New York Governor Horatio Seymour in 1868, Grant failed to carry New York, but he won the state against *New York Tribune* editor Horace Greeley in 1872. Grant moved to Manhattan in 1881 and spent his final days writing his memoirs in Wilton, Saratoga County. He died in 1885.

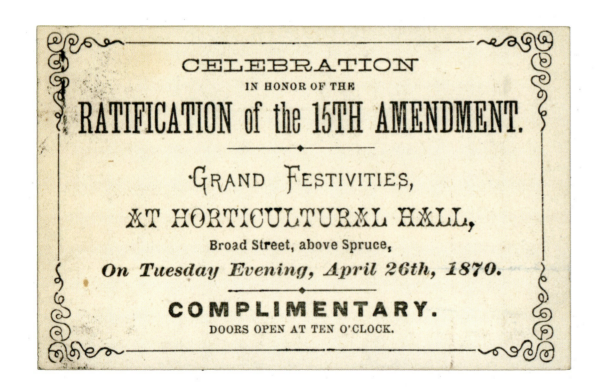

TICKET TO THE CELEBRATION IN HONOR OF THE RATIFICATION OF THE 15TH AMENDMENT, WASHINGTON D.C., 1870
Despite the Fifteenth Amendment, which allowed black men to vote, many states had strict voter eligibility laws including literacy tests and poll taxes. *(Courtesy of Elizabeth Meaders)*

WICKER CHAIR, WAKEFIELD RATTAN COMPANY, NEW YORK, 1885
This chair was purchased for the Grant family prior to their stay at the cottage in Wilton. President Grant arrived at the cottage on June 16, 1885, with a large entourage of family, friends, servants, and physicians in order to complete his memoirs. He died just four days after his final proofreading.
(New York State Parks, Recreation and Historic Preservation)

GEN. U.S. GRANT, WRITING HIS MEMOIRS AT MT. McGREGOR, JUNE 27, 1885 PHOTO BY HOWE? N.Y. © DEC. 2, 1886 - CP. P15684

GRANT IN CHAIR
Image of Ulysses S. Grant working on his memoirs in Wilton, Saratoga County. In 1889, the Mount McGregor Memorial Association bought the cottage in which Grant died. New York State assumed ownership of the site in 1957.
(New York State Parks, Recreation and Historic Preservation)

Remembering the War
Memorialization

After 1877, both Northerners and Southerners devoted themselves to reconciling their differences rather than reconstructing society. They celebrated soldiers from both sides in art, literature, and popular culture. The G.A.R. did its part to bring people together by holding annual "National Encampments" for both U.S. and Confederate veterans through 1949. New Yorkers, too, commemorated the heroism and valor of the men who fought by building memorials in town squares, across the New York landscape, and on battlefields in other states.

MODEL, MONUMENT TO THE 122ND NEW YORK VOLUNTEER INFANTRY REGIMENT
The 122nd New York Volunteer Infantry was known as the "Onondagas," because it was raised in Onondaga County. This model is a replica of one that the State of New York dedicated on the Gettysburg Battlefield dedicated in 1888. The monument is topped by the cross that is the symbol of the Union 6th Army Corps and is fronted with a bronze of the Seal of the State of New York. *(Onondaga Historical Association)*

REMEMBERING THE WAR, *left*
Members of the 43rd New York Infantry at the monument dedication, ca. 1889. *(Alan Shineman)*

231

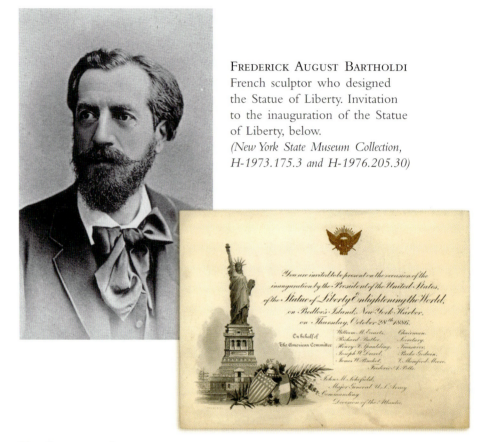

FREDERICK AUGUST BARTHOLDI
French sculptor who designed the Statue of Liberty. Invitation to the inauguration of the Statue of Liberty, below.
(New York State Museum Collection, H-1973.175.3 and H-1976.205.30)

THE STATUE OF LIBERTY
French political activists, opposed to slavery and at odds with Napoleon III's authoritarian regime at home, initially conceived of the Statue of Liberty as a monument to emancipation and the triumph the Union's democratic form of government over one dominated by aristocratic Southern plantation owners. When the Statue was dedicated in 1886, the president of the Union League Club, Chauncey M. Depew, closed the ceremonies with a lengthy speech commemorating the shared French-American devotion to freedom. He noted that "the development of Liberty was impossible while she was shackled to a slave." Over time, the Statue came to symbolize freedom for immigrants seeking a better life in America.
(New York State Museum Collection, H-1973.175.3)

GETTYSBURG REUNION
Veterans at the 50th Reunion of the Battle of Gettysburg.
(New York State Archives)

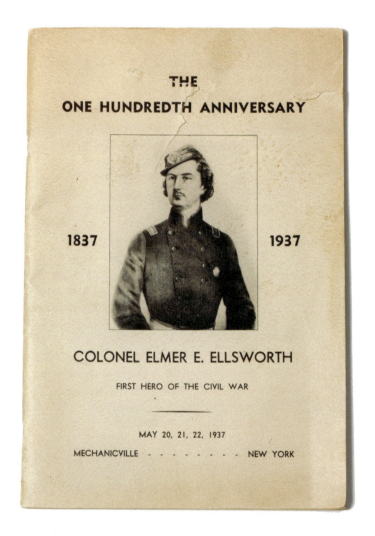

BOOK, 1937
The publication celebrates the 100th birthday of Colonel Elmer Ellsworth, the first U.S. officer killed in the Civil War. Ellsworth grew up and is buried in Mechanicville, Saratoga County. *(Courtesy of Stephanie Miller)*

LINCOLN DOORSTOP
Objects celebrating Lincoln, such as this doorstop, were popular long after his death. *(Bernard Margolis)*

STONEWARE JUG, HAXTUN OTTMAN & CO., FORT EDWARD, N.Y., C.1867
This three-gallon jug is decorated with a bearded man in a basket. It is possibly a memorial to Abraham Lincoln. Lincoln memorials were popular for decades after his death.
(New York State Museum, Weitsman Stoneware Collection, H-2006.52.6)

SOLDIERS' AND SAILORS' ARCH, GRAND ARMY PLAZA, BROOKLYN, 1891
The Soldiers' and Sailors' Arch is dedicated "To the Defenders of the Union, 1861–1865" *(Library of Congress)*

77TH INFANTRY REGIMENT MONUMENT, C. 1900
Congress Park, Saratoga Springs, Saratoga County *(Library of Congress)*

237

1864 — 1865

U.S.A.   C.S.A.

Dedication
of the
Elmira
Prison Camp
Monument

Aug. 25, 1985
Elmira, N.Y.

COLLECTION OF CIVIL WAR MEMENTOES, *right*
The war made a lasting impression on David Knight, Company D, 8th New York Volunteer Calvary, who enlisted on September 16, 1861. He collected and assembled each of these mementoes from his engagements during the Civil War. Knight was wounded near Snickers Gap, Virginia, on June 18, 1863, and was discharged at Washington on July 14, 1863.
(New York State Museum Collection, H-2013.14.1)

RIBBON, 1985
This ribbon commemorates the dedication of the Elmira Prison Camp Monument in 1985. The Elmira Prison Camp held over 12,500 Confederate soldiers between 1864 and 1865. More than twenty-five percent of these prisoners died while detained at the prison.
(Chemung County Historical Society)

MINIATURE SOLDIERS, CAST METAL, PAINTED, C.1950
Civil War miniatures have long been popular with children and hobbyists—and this was particularly the case during the war's Centennial, 1961–65.
(New York State Museum Collection, H-1967.2.85)

239

GENERAL GRANT'S TOMB
(Library of Congress/J.S. Johnston, View & Marine Photo)

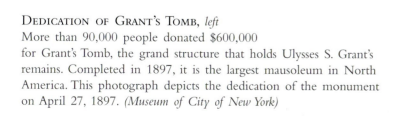

DEDICATION OF GRANT'S TOMB, *left*
More than 90,000 people donated $600,000
for Grant's Tomb, the grand structure that holds Ulysses S. Grant's
remains. Completed in 1897, it is the largest mausoleum in North
America. This photograph depicts the dedication of the monument
on April 27, 1897. *(Museum of City of New York)*

GRANT TOMB DEDICATION, VIEW OF GRANT'S TOMB
Claremont Heights, New York City in background and Dolphny,
U.S.N. ship, and tugboats in foreground.
(Library of Congress/J.S. Johnston, View & Marine Photo)

Al Smith The Negro Lover

A Vital Message to Alabama Democracy

SMITH'S RECORD AGAINST WHITE SUPREMACY

The liquor daily press has repeatedly raised the negro question in its attempt to stem the tide of Democratic revolt against Al Smith.

With John J. Raskob, a lifelong Republican, as Chairman of the National Committee, and Al Smith, a tool of Tammany, as nominee, we must consider this question with care, and not accept the biased view of highly partisan newspapers.

Al Smith is the worst foe of "White Supremacy" in public life in the United States today.

Ferdinand Q. Morton, a negro, is one of three commissioners of New York City. As such, he has under him white girls, white women and white men, as well as colored people. He, along with two others, has charge of Tammany Hall patronage, and has charge of the employing and discharging of men and women in New York City.

The appointment of this negro was a reward for the constant support of Al Smith by the negro population of New York.

Negro women in large numbers have been appointed inspectors in New York. These negro inspectors go into white as well as colored homes and have authority thereover.

NEGROES IN SCHOOLS

White and black children are indiscriminately mixed in the public schools of New York. Little white children in schools where the majority of the pupils are colored have consistently been refused the right to transfer to white schools. Negro teachers in large numbers are employed. The negro teachers teach white as well as colored children.

AL SMITH HAS MADE IT A CRIME TO SEPARATE NEGROES AND WHITES

The New York Legislature of 1913 passed a bill making it a crime in New York for the owner or proprietor of any dance hall, bath house or other place of amusement or accommodation to separate white girls and boys from the negro men and women.

Al Smith was Speaker of the House that passed this bill. He voted for it and helped to pass it. (We are attaching this bill in full for you to read).

EQUAL RIGHTS IN PLACES OF PUBLIC ACCOMMODATION, RESORT OR AMUSEMENT.—All persons within the jurisdiction of this state shall be entitled to the full and equal accommodations, advantages and privileges of any place of public accommodation, resort or amusement, subject only to the conditions and limitations established by law and applicable alike to all persons. No person, being the owner, lessee, proprietor, manager, superintendent, agent or employee of any such place, shall directly or indirectly refuse, withhold from or deny to any person any of the accommodations, advantages or privileges thereof, or directly or indirectly publish, circulate, issue, display, post or mail any written or printed communication, notice or advertisement, to the effect that any such place shall be refused, withheld from or denied to any person on account of race creed or color, or that the patronage or custom thereat, of any person belonging to or purporting to be of any particular race, creed or color is unwelcome, objectionable or not acceptable, desired or solicited. The production of any such written or printed communication, notice or advertisement, purporting to relate to any such place and to be made by any person being the owner, lessee, proprietor, superintendent or manager thereof, shall be presumptive evidence in any civil or criminal action that the same was authorized by such person. A place of public accommodation, resort or amusement within the meaning of this article, shall be deemed to include any inn, tavern or hotel, whether conducted for the entertainment of transient guests, or for the accommodation of those seeking health, recreation or rest, any restaurant, eating-house, public conveyance on land or water, bath-house, barber-shop, theater and music hall. Nothing herein contained shall be construed to prohibit the mailing of a private communication in writing sent in response to a specific written inquiry.

The second section reads as follows:

PENALTY FOR VIOLATION.—Any person who shall violate any of the provisions of the foregoing section, or who shall aid or incite the violation of any of said provisions shall for each and every violation thereof be liable to a penalty of not less than one hundred dollars nor more than five hundred dollars, to be recovered by the person aggrieved thereby or by any resident of this state, to whom such person shall assign his cause of action, in any court of competent jurisdiction in the county in which the plaintiff or defendant shall reside; and shall, also, for every such offense be deemed guilty of a misdemeanor, and upon conviction thereof shall be fined not less than one hundred dollars nor more than five hundred dollars, or shall be imprisoned not less than thirty days nor more than ninety days, or both such fine and imprisonment.

The third section reads as follows:

This Act shall take effect September first, nineteen hundred and thirteen.

Al Smith passed this bill to catch the negro vote.

MARRIAGE OF NEGROES AND WHITES

In the same year, with Al Smith still occupying the position of Speaker of the House, a bill amending the penal code and "prohibiting the inter-marriage or cohabitation of white persons and negroes" never saw the light of day. The bill was never reported out of committee and no action whatever was ever taken upon it.

Tammany had two-thirds of both branches of the Legislature and Alfred E. Smith, the man who now claims to be a Jeffersonian Democrat, was Speaker of the Assembly.

NOW READ THIS

United States Senator Royal S. Copeland, of New York is quoted as follows on Smith's standing with the negroes:

"I have long known his strength with them (negroes) in New York state and find he is strong with them in Ohio, Indiana and Illinois where the colored people hold the balance of how these states will go this fall."

Senator Copeland, Democrat Senator from New York, issued a statement last Thursday in which he virtually acknowledged the Tammany-Democratic party to be the party of the negro for the present campaign.

Jimmie Walker Tammany Mayor of New York, addressing a meeting of the Colored Business Men of New York said: "Gentlemen, after Nov. 6, your people will be as welcome in the White House (the home of the President) as you are now welcome in New York."

Can Alabama Democrats permit Al Smith to use them, while catering to the Northern negro?

Does party regularity mean more to you than the purity of the white race?

We are not quitting the Democratic Party. We are just detouring around Al Smith, a mud hole, on the Democratic Highway.

Let's rid Democracy of the "Damnable affliction of Tammany Hall."

"Let Us Dare to Do Right"

Paid political advertisement by Anti-Al Smith Democratic Headquarters, Hugh A. Locke, Chairman, 310 Jackson Building, Birmingham, Ala.

Retreat from Reconstruction

Following Reconstruction, state and federal governments enabled racial discrimination for the better part of a century. Former Confederate states passed laws requiring "separate but equal" status for African Americans. In effect, this resulted in the legal segregation of schools, rest rooms, and restaurants. New Yorkers, meanwhile, focused their energies on expanding their businesses and industries—not on social justice—and New York and other Northern states allowed *de facto* segregation through unfair housing, biased lending practices, and job discrimination.

Racial prejudice remained strong, and more than a few New Yorkers forgot why they had fought the war. Some even accepted the Southern myth (known as the "Lost Cause") that slavery was a benevolent institution and that Northern aggression had caused the war. These ideas became popular, in part, because of films such as *Birth of a Nation* (1915) and *Gone with the Wind* (1939).

AL SMITH THE NEGRO LOVER, BROADSIDE
Racists in Alabama and elsewhere opposed New York Governor Al Smith's candidacy for the presidency in 1928. Smith had promoted a pro-civil rights agenda and led the fight against the Ku Klux Klan in New York. *(New York State Archives)*

The Ku Klux Klan in New York

In the early 1920s, more than 200,000 New Yorkers formed Ku Klux Klan (KKK) chapters all over the state. The KKK had been founded as an often violent vigilante group in 1865 to restrict African American freedoms in Tennessee. KKK membership soon spread to other former Confederate states. After 1915, however, the Klan moved north, not just in opposition to black equality, but to Catholic and Jewish immigration. The movement declined in 1923 after passage of the *Walker Law*. This required membership organizations in New York to reveal their oaths and bylaws and to turn over their membership lists.

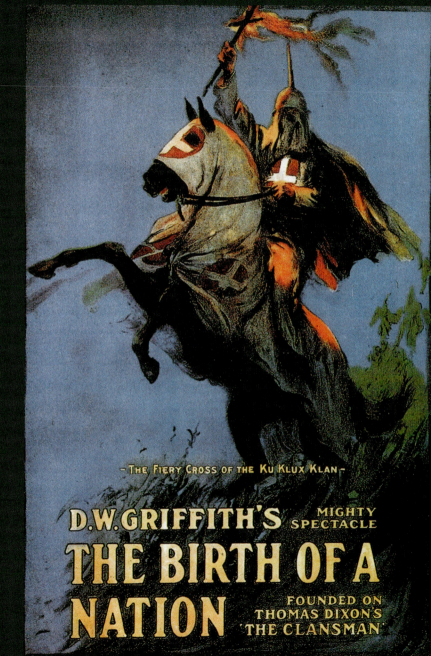

BIRTH OF A NATION THEATRICAL POSTER
Birth of a Nation, released in 1915, was used as a recruiting tool for the KKK. *(Chronicle of the Cinema)*

KKK PARADE IN BINGHAMTON, NEW YORK, 1924
The Klan's New York state headquarters was located in Binghamton.
(Broome County Historical Society)

KKK ROBE AND HOOD, C. 1920
This Klan robe and hood are from
Greene County.
(New York State Museum Collection,
H-1983.136)

October 28, 1938

Motion Picture Division,
State Education Department,
New York, New York

Gentlemen:

 Will you please send to us the license number under which the motion picture "The Birth of a Nation," is being shown?

 Will you also please outline to us the procedure for applying for the cancellation of this permit?

Yours very truly,

Thurgood Marshall
Assistant Special Counsel

TM:AG

LETTER, OCTOBER 28, 1938

Thurgood Marshall wrote this letter on behalf of the NAACP in an effort to stop the screening of the movie, *Birth of a Nation,* in New York City. *Birth of a Nation* is a 1915 silent film that chronicles the relationships of two families (one Northern and one Southern) during the Civil War and Reconstruction. The film was controversial, because it portrayed African American men poorly and glorified the Ku Klux Klan. The NAACP was unsuccessful in banning the movie in New York City. Similar demonstrations, sponsored by the NAACP, occurred across New York State and the nation.

(New York State Archives)

The Continuing Struggle for Equality

Many New Yorkers continued to resist the erosion of civil rights throughout the late-nineteenth and mid-twentieth centuries. Frederick Douglass remained a national civil rights spokesman until his death in 1895. W.E.B. Du Bois and others founded the pro-civil rights Niagara Movement in and around Buffalo in 1905. Four years later, movement members joined with white progressives to form the National Association for the Advancement for Colored People (NAACP) in Manhattan. Soon after, Marcus Garvey developed a huge but short-lived following in support of black self-determination and economic development.

FOUNDERS OF THE NIAGARA MOVEMENT
Founders of the Niagara Movement met in Ontario, Canada, in 1905, because hotels on the U.S. side of the Falls barred blacks. The group disagreed sharply with Booker T. Washington's willingness to compromise with Jim Crow supporters.
(Library of Congress)

LYNCHING BANNER

The NAACP flew this flag from its 5th Avenue headquarters in New York City whenever a man or woman was lynched. Nearly 3,500 lynchings of African Americans took place in the U.S. from 1882 through 1968 (there were also approximately 1,300 lynchings of whites). This picture was taken in 1936. *(Library of Congress)*

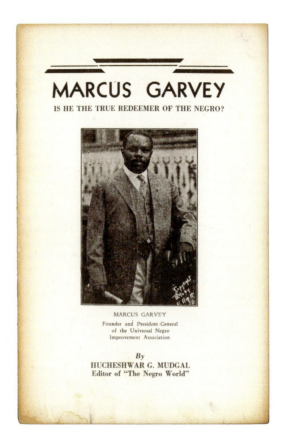

MARCUS GARVEY: IS HE THE TRUE REDEEMER OF THE NEGRO?
1932 PAMPHLET
Garvey and the Universal Negro Improvement Association (UNIA) published the newspaper *Negro World*. All of the articles were specifically aimed at people of African ancestry. The paper had a distribution of 500,000 a week at its peak in the 1920s.
(New York State Museum Collection, H-2010.45.26)

DOUGLASS MONUMENT, ROCHESTER, MONROE COUNTY
The monument to Frederick Douglass was unveiled June 9, 1899. Rochester was home to the Douglass family for many years. Douglass also published his newspaper, *The North Star*, in Rochester. This was one of the first monuments in the United States dedicated to an African American.
(Albert R. Stone Negative Collection, Rochester Museum & Science Center)

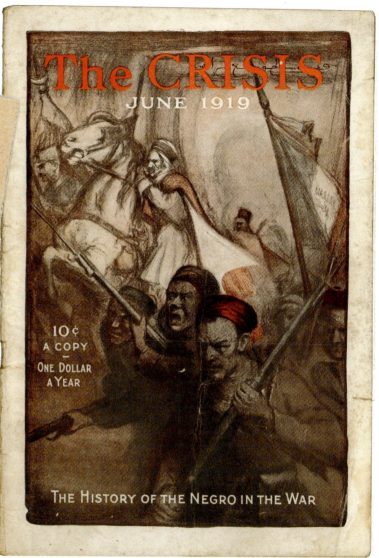

UNIA DUES CARD AND MEMBERSHIP PIN, C. 1923
With over two million members by 1920, Marcus Garvey's UNIA (headquartered in Harlem) had a profound worldwide political and cultural influence on people of African descent. Garvey demanded basic civil rights, political and judicial equality, racial self-determination, and the political unification of African peoples everywhere. He was a controversial figure who was convicted of mail fraud and deported to Jamaica in 1927.
(New York State Museum Collection, H-2010.45.3)

The Crisis, JUNE 1919
The Crisis was the official publication of the NAACP and was founded in 1910 by W.E.B. Du Bois, who served as editor until 1934. *The Crisis* was predominately a news journal, but also included poems, reviews, and essays on culture and history.
(New York State Museum Collection, H-2010.45.28)

A Second Reconstruction

Many African Americans and some whites renewed demands for equality after World War II. President Truman integrated the U.S. Armed Forces (1948), and in New York, Jackie Robinson integrated Major League Baseball (1947). In 1954, in a case argued by Thurgood Marshall before the United States Supreme Court, the NAACP won the landmark *Brown v. Board of Education* decision that paved the way for the Civil Rights Movement of the 1950s and 60s. Initially, the Civil Rights Movement was characterized by non-violent resistance and civil disobedience, later by black militancy.

In New York, church organizations, race groups, and college students fought discrimination in the South and at home. In the first half of the twentieth century, African American migrants from the South poured into New York State's cities only

Thurgood Marshall, 1957
Future Supreme Court Justice Thurgood Marshall served as Chief Counsel for the NAACP between 1936 and 1961—during which time he won 29 of the 32 cases he argued before the Supreme Court. *(Photograph by Thomas J. O'Halloran, Library of Congress)*

Among the lawyers recruited to fight Jim Crow in public schools were (*left to right*): Elmwood H. Chisholm, Oliver W. Hill, Marshall, Spottswood W. Robinson III, Harold Boulware of South Carolina, and Jack Greenberg.

JACKIE ROBINSON (1919–72)

Jackie Robinson is one of the most culturally and politically significant athletes in American history. He became the first African American to play major league baseball when he made his debut with the Brooklyn Dodgers in 1947. This effectively ended the segregation that had relegated black players to the Negro Leagues since the 1880s. Robinson succeeded, not only because of his outstanding athletic ability, but because of his strong character and determination to make a lasting difference. *(Library of Congress)*

WOMAN SEWING PARACHUTES, UNITED STATES OFFICE OF WAR INFORMATION, 1943

In 1942, the Roosevelt administration issued Executive Order 8802 banning racial discrimination in the war industries. The United States Office of War Information used this photo in the book, *Negroes and the War*, in an effort to recruit more African Americans to the war effort. Blacks served in both the military and on the home front. The modern civil rights movement matured after WWII, when many African Americans who had served with honor in the war were no longer willing to accept racial discrimination and injustice from a country they fought so hard to defend. *(New York State Museum Collection, H-2010.45.24)*

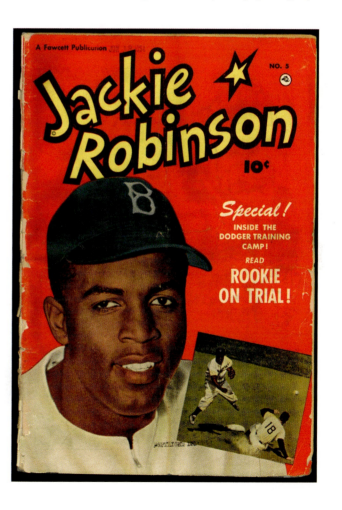

SHIRLEY CHISHOLM CAMPAIGN POSTER, 1972
Shirley Chisholm (1924–2005) began her political career as a state assembly representative in 1964. Four years later, she became the first African American woman elected to the United States Congress representing Brooklyn's Bedford-Stuyvesant district. She served there for fourteen years focusing especially on education, labor, and veterans' and women's issues. In 1972, she was the first woman to run for the Democratic nomination for the U.S. presidency. *(New York State Museum Collection, H-2010.41.1)*

to find racially restrictive real estate covenants that kept them from purchasing or renting homes in desirable neighborhoods, few employment opportunities, and in many areas, overall *de facto* segregation. Local chapters of the NAACP and the Congress on Racial Equality (CORE) worked with local organizers to bring equality to all New Yorkers.

> "When I die, I want to be remembered as a woman who lived in the 20th century and who dared to be a catalyst of change. I don't want to be remembered as the first black woman who went to Congress. And I don't even want to be remembered as the first woman who happened to be black to make the bid for the presidency. I want to be remembered as a woman who fought for change in the 20th century. That's what I want."
>
> —*Shirley Chisholm*

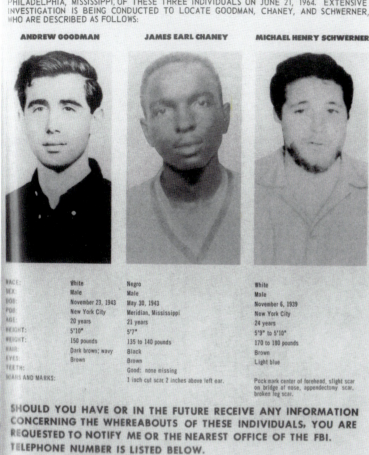

MISSING POSTER

THE FBI IS SEEKING INFORMATION CONCERNING THE DISAPPEARANCE AT PHILADELPHIA, MISSISSIPPI, OF THESE THREE INDIVIDUALS ON JUNE 21, 1964. EXTENSIVE INVESTIGATION IS BEING CONDUCTED TO LOCATE GOODMAN, CHANEY, AND SCHWERNER, WHO ARE DESCRIBED AS FOLLOWS:

In 1964, KKK members in Mississippi lynched three Civil Rights workers: a 21-year-old Mississippi black man, James Chaney, and two white New Yorkers, 20-year-old student Andrew Goodman and 24-year-old CORE activist Michael Schwerner. The murders went unpunished until 2005, when after several failed prosecutions, a Mississippi court convicted local minister Edgar Ray Killen of manslaughter.
(Federal Bureau of Investigation)

STAINED GLASS MEMORIAL

Goodman, Chaney, and Schwerner died in the South fighting for the same freedoms for which New Yorkers and other Americans had sacrificed their lives a century earlier. This stained glass memorial was installed on the Cornell University campus at Sage Chapel by the Cornell Class of 1961. Michael Schwerner and both of Andrew Goodman's parents were Cornell graduates. *(Cornell University)*

JOIN THE MARCH
TO PROTEST THE BOMBINGS OF BIRMINGHAM

WE PROTEST . . .

- The murder of six children in Birmingham
- Twenty-one unsolved bombings against Negro homes and businesses
- The actions of irresponsible elected officials
- The inaction of "responsible" citizens

MEET

Place: All Souls' Unitarian Church—16th and Harvard Streets, N.W.
Date: Sunday, September 22, 1963
Time: 2 P.M.
Route: Down 16th Street to Lafayette Park (opposite the White House) OR:
You may join the march at Scott Circle (16th and Mass. Ave.) at 3 P.M.
and continue to the White House from that point.

BLACK ARM BANDS TO BE DISTRIBUTED

Washington D.C. Congress of Racial Equality, CORE

Join the March, HANDBILL, 1963
(Courtesy of Elizabeth Meaders)

CORE ACTIVISTS
CORE activists protesting unfair housing at a rally in New York City, 1964.
(Library of Congress, NYWT&S Collection)

CIVIL RIGHTS ORGANIZATION PROTEST PINS, C. 1960S AND 1970S
(New York State Museum History Collections and Elizabeth Meaders)

CORE HAT, C.1963
CORE was founded in Chicago in 1942 and later headquartered in New York City. The foundation of CORE's program was non-violent direct action to promote social justice and racial equality. CORE organized protests and demonstrations in both the South and the North. *(New York State Museum Collection, H-2012.12.2)*

CIVIL RIGHTS ORGANIZATION PROTEST PINS, C. 1960S AND 1970S
(New York State Museum History Collections and Elizabeth Meaders)

BULLET HOLES AT AUDUBON BALLROOM FOLLOWING THE
ASSASSINATION OF MALCOLM X
(Library of Congress)

CHAIR FROM THE AUDUBON BALLROOM
(New York State Museum Collection, H-2007.76.1)

COMMEMORATION DAY IN HONOR OF MALCOLM X, BROADSIDE, 1966

Organizers planned this march to commemorate the 1965 assassination of Malcolm X by members of the Nation of Islam. Malcolm was a spokesman for the group in the 1950s and 60s, but he came to reject its message of black supremacy. He broke with the Nation of Islam in 1964 and expressed his willingness to work more closely with other civil rights leaders. The march began at the Audubon Ballroom in Harlem—the place where Malcolm was killed.
(New York State Museum Collection, H-2010.45.2)

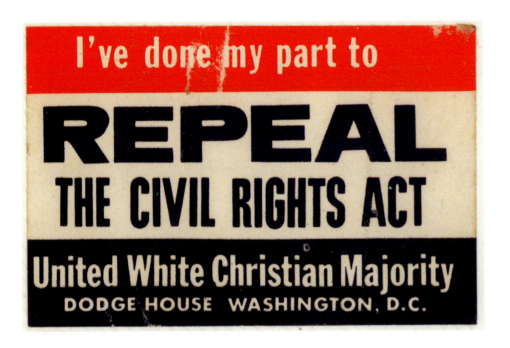

REPEAL THE CIVIL RIGHTS ACT, HANDBILL, 1964
(Courtesy of Elizabeth Meaders)

SOCIETY FOR THE PREVENTION OF NEGROES GETTING EVERYTHING
(SPONGE), BUSINESS CARD, NEW YORK CITY, C. 1967
(Courtesy of Elizabeth Meaders)

ANTI-CIVIL RIGHTS MATERIAL
Organized groups in New York and across the country continued to work against civil rights, even as the movement gained momentum in the 1960s. Anti-black feelings peaked in the 1970s when blacks made advances in the work force and whites feared the loss of employment as a result. These feelings were exacerbated by soldiers returning from the Vietnam War in large numbers and re-entering an economy that was in a recession in the 1970s.

New York State's Civil War Centennial Celebration

On April 12, 1960, Governor Nelson A. Rockefeller signed legislation that created the fifteen-member New York State Civil War Centennial Commission. The commission was chaired by Civil War historian Bruce Catton and co-chaired by John Hope Franklin (at the time the most pre-eminent African American historian in the U.S.). In addition to the parades, re-enactments, and observances that the commission organized, Governor Rockefeller, a liberal Republican and civil rights champion, wanted to demonstrate his support for the emerging Civil Rights movement. The Governor's emphasis on slavery and emancipation distinguished New York's Centennial commemorations from the celebrations of battles, battlefields, and regional heritage that were taking place across the South. Ultimately, the New York's Centennial Commission helped give the Civil War new meaning to Americans everywhere.

"We can best observe the Centennial of the Civil War by redoubling our efforts to complete the task begun by those who fought and died to preserve the Union, eradicate the barbarism of slavery, and establish equal rights for all people."

—John Hope Franklin at the opening ceremonies of the New York Civil War Centennial Commission, April 17, 1961

Archbishop of New York Cardinal Francis Joseph Spellman, Dr. Martin Luther King Jr., and Governor Nelson A. Rockefeller at the emancipation dinner in NYC
(New York State Archives)

"There is but one way to commemorate the Emancipation Proclamation. That is to make its declarations of freedom real. . . . and reaffirm democracy by deeds as bold and daring as the issuance of the Emancipation Proclamation."

—*Dr. Martin Luther King Jr.,*
September 12, 1962, NYC

IMAGE OF THE PROPOSED EMANCIPATION PROCLAMATION SHRINE
In 1962, Governor Rockefeller sought to pass legislation establishing a commission to design a permanent New York State shrine to house the Preliminary Emancipation Proclamation. Funding never materialized. *(New York State Archives)*

Page 1 (left manuscript):

[handwritten at top] I need not pause to say how very delighted I am to be here this evening and to be a part of this auspicious occasion.

ADDRESS OF THE REVEREND DR. MARTIN LUTHER KING, JR.
New York State Civil War Centennial Commission - Park Sheraton
Hotel, New York City - Wednesday Evening, September 12, 1962

Mankind through the ages has been in a ceaseless struggle to give dignity and meaning to human life. It is that quest which separates it from the *[handwritten: distinguishes man / lower]* animals, whose biological functions and anatomical features resemble aspects of the human specie. *[handwritten: Not used]*

[handwritten: Start:]

If our nation had done nothing more in its whole history than to create just two documents, its contribution to civilization would be imperishable. The first of these documents is the Declaration of Independence and the other is that which we are here today to honor, *[handwritten: tonight]* the Emancipation Proclamation. All tyrants, past, present and future, are powerless to bury the truths in these declarations, no matter how extensive their legions, how vast their power and how malignant their evil.

The Declaration of Independence proclaimed to a world, organized politically and spiritually around the concept of the inequality of man, that the liberty and dignity of human personality were inherent in man as a living being, that he, himself, could not create a society which could last if it alienated freedom from man. The Emancipation Proclamation was the offspring of the Declaration of Independence using the forces of law to uproot a social order which sought to separate liberty from a segment of humanity. The principle of equality on which the nation was founded had to be

[handwritten: It was a constructive use of the force]

Page 2 (right manuscript):

- 2 -

reaffirmed in the flames of a scorching war until rededication to liberty was once again recorded in the Emancipation Proclamation.

Our pride and our progress could be unqualified if the story might end here. But history reveals that these *[handwritten: America has been a ? phrenic personality when these two documents are concerned. On the one hand she has proudly professed the basic principles inherent in both documents. On the other hand she has sadly practiced the antithesis of these principles.]* documents were each to live lives of stormy contradictions, to be both observed and violated through social upheavals and spiritual disasters.

If we look at our history with honesty and clarity we will be forced to admit that our Federal form of government has been, from the day of its birth, weakened in its integrity, confused and confounded in its direction, by the unresolved race question. It is as if a political thalidamide drug taken during pregnancy caused the birth of a crippled nation. We seldom take note or give adequate significance to the fact that Thomas Jefferson's text of the Declaration of Independence was revised by the Continental Congress to eliminate a justifiable attack on King George for encouraging slave trade. It was expunged *[handwritten: changed]* lest it offend the southern representatives, just as today, still, legislation is discarded or emasculated lest it, too, give offense to southern representatives. Jefferson knew that such compromises with principle struck at the heart of the nation's security and integrity. In 1820, 6 years before his death, he wrote these melancholy words,

---

DR. MARTIN LUTER KING JR. DELIVERING A SPEECH AT THE EMANCIPATION PROCLAMATION DINNER (*left*) **AND TWO PAGES FROM DR. KING'S SPEECH** (*above*)
When Governor Rockefeller hosted his 1962 Emancipation Proclamation Dinner in New York City, he invited Dr. Martin Luther King Jr., to attend it. Dr. King initially had a scheduling conflict, and he and his advisors were concerned that the event might be perceived as too partisan. Rockefeller was a Republican, and King did not want to risk losing the Democratic support he needed for his civil rights agenda (particularly from President John F. Kennedy). Dr. King overcame his misgivings when he recognized that the Centennial Commission was more bipartisan than he had originally thought and that many of the governor's wealthy friends would be present at the dinner. He was likely influenced, too, by the fact that Rockefeller had made a donation to help rebuild African American churches that had been burned in Georgia. (*New York State Archives*)

The Civil War in the Twenty-first Century

Like many Americans, New Yorkers today are as fascinated by the Civil War as they were in the 1960s. Thousands travel widely to participate in battle re-enactments. Others collect Civil War memorabilia, research their Civil War ancestry, and join Civil War Roundtables.

At the same time, both New York and the rest of the nation have changed considerably since the Civil War Centennial and the early days of the Civil Rights movement. There has been substantial social, political, and cultural progress, but many of the same issues that troubled New Yorkers fifty years ago remain unresolved today. Never-ending debates associated with the war continue. Was John Brown a martyr or a terrorist? What is the legacy of slavery? How do we define American freedom? Does government guarantee or threaten that freedom? How do Americans resolve their differences and maintain a strong union? Was the Civil War an "irrepressible conflict," or could it have been prevented?

Cub Scouts at the 2011 rededication of the Ellsworth Memorial, Mechanicville, Saratoga County
(Maryellen Albanese)

Index